The Man Who Sees
Dead People

Joe Power became aware of his psychic abilities when he was a very young child. As he grew up he discovered he was clairvoyant, clairaudient and clairessient and, in addition, that he was able to communicate with the spirit world. But it was not until his brother was found dead and Joe encountered him in the spirit world that he decided to embrace his talent. For the last ten years, Joe has studied and practised psychic mediumship, giving private readings and public demonstrations. He has appeared on numerous television and radio shows, and has been featured in many magazines and newspaper articles. Joe has run psychic/medium teaching courses all over the UK, and has also taught alongside tutors at the world-famous Arthur Findlay College. He has a special interest in using his extraordinary powers to investigate unsolved crimes around the world. Joe lives in Liverpool.

American Jill Wellington has been a journalist for thirty years, including fourteen years as an award-winning television news reporter in Michigan. She has reported for radio and written a weekly humour column for her local newspaper. Jill is also a freelance magazine writer for metaphysical magazines all over the world. She and her mother, Edna Mae Holm, are the co-authors of the mystery novel *Fireworks* that teaches the concept of synchronicity or meaningful coincidences.

The Man Who Sees Dead People

JOE POWER

As told to Jill Wellington

PENGUIN BOOKS

PENGUIN BOOKS

Published by the Penguin Group
Penguin Books Ltd, 80 Strand, London WC2R ORL, England
Penguin Group (USA) Inc., 375 Hudson Street, New York, New York 10014, USA
Penguin Group (Canada), 90 Eglinton Avenue East, Suite 700, Toronto, Ontario, Canada M4P 2Y3
(a division of Pearson Penguin Canada Inc.)
Penguin Ireland, 25 St Stephen's Green, Dublin 2, Ireland (a division of Penguin Books Ltd)
Penguin Group (Australia), 250 Camberwell Road, Camberwell, Victoria 3124, Australia
(a division of Pearson Australia Group Pty Ltd)
Penguin Books India Pvt Ltd, 11 Community Centre, Panchsheel Park, New Delhi – 110 017, India
Penguin Group (NZ), 67 Apollo Drive, Rosedale, North Shore 0632, New Zealand
(a division of Pearson New Zealand Ltd)
Penguin Books (South Africa) (Pty) Ltd, 24 Sturdee Avenue,
Rosebank, Johannesburg 2196, South Africa

Penguin Books Ltd, Registered Offices: 80 Strand, London WC2R ORL, England

www.penguin.com

First published 2009

3

Northamptonshire Libraries & Information Service
DV

Askews	

ISBN: 978-0-141-04042-4

www.greenpenguin.co.uk

This book is dedicated to my brother Denny on the tenth anniversary of his crossing. His memory still makes me laugh. I miss you, Denny, but you are still an important part of my journey.

I

I was born at the Liverpool Royal Hospital on 24 September 1966, the same year that a psychic told John Lennon he would be shot in America. I sensed from a very early age that I was somehow different. People generally say that they have little or no memory of infancy or toddlerhood. I, on the other hand, was very conscious of my surroundings and the people around me from the start, and now realize that this heightened awareness was an early indication of my psychic sensibility. I remember lots of incidents from my early childhood extremely vividly.

The autumn air was crisp the day of my first memory. I was two months old and remember feeling smothered by the weight of blankets bearing down on me in my pram. My mother, Sandra, was taking me to her sister's, a mile down the road from our house in Liverpool. I remember Aunt Carla plucking me from the pram and the wetness of her kiss, and the disgusting smell that assaulted me when we went into what must have been the living room. The room was gloomy and decorated in the style of the era. There was a fireplace with a wood surround and, within it, an old gas fire behind a metal grille. There was a vase shaped like an owl on a wobbly table with one leg shorter than the others that held a bouquet of dying flowers. In one corner, yellowing newspapers had been heaped up. Even in my infant mind, I remember wondering if they hid a patch of worn carpet. The smell grew stronger. In later years, I was to realize what it was: the horrible smell of glue and leather. Uncle Norman had a side job, common in those days as a way of making ends meet, gluing chamois leathers together to earn a few extra bob.

I was crying, and Auntie Carla passed me over to him. My crying didn't stop when he cooed at me and pinched my cheeks. I remember being frightened when he tossed me into the air, but I could still sense his love for me. It was so strong, I felt the loss of it whenever he left the room. Underneath this affection, though, I sensed an atmosphere of melancholy and misery permeating the entire house, mingling with the stench of leather and glue. Even at the age of two months, my mind was finely tuned to what was going on around me. Shortly afterwards, Auntie Carla and Uncle Norman split up.

I was christened Joseph Patrick Power. My Christian name was given to me by my Great-aunt Emmie. Six months before my birth, she cornered Mum. Even though she was tiny, you couldn't ignore her presence. Her piercing eyes commanded attention.

'You must name this little one Joseph,' she said firmly, 'because he is the fourth child.' Mum had no idea what she meant, but she followed Great-aunt Emmie's orders and named me Joseph.

Great-aunt Emmie is part of my psychic heritage. She was considered a great psychic in her time and enjoyed some celebrity around Liverpool because she could read tea leaves. She could also also predict the winners at the horse races, so all the locals would visit her when they wanted a bit of a flutter. She wasn't very popular with the bookies, but what could they do? It wasn't as if she was cheating.

She died shortly after I was born. The bookies were relieved, but she and her psychic abilities were missed and lived on in local memory for years to come.

I was the youngest of four children born to Mum and my father, Jackie Power. We lived in a house in Bootle's Marion Square, which overlooked a church called Holy Spirit. When I was an infant, Mum used to take me for walks, pushing me in my pram, and we would pass it. I always felt as if I was somehow being taunted when we drew near and I would burst into tears. My mother couldn't figure out what was the matter with me and was unable to stop me crying.

I later found out that the church was said to be home to a ghost, who would stalk the streets and wander into the houses near by. People were terrified by the stories. I wonder now if I was sensitive to spirits even then. When I was a bit older, I remember I used to take a careful look at the church before I ever went in and, once in there, I always had a strange feeling, which would come over me in waves.

*

At two years old, I understood what 'Power' meant. My father lived up to his surname, and then some. Sometimes he fought with Mum and made life difficult for my older brother, Tommy, my two sisters, Tracey and Diane, and me.

I often felt defenceless in that house, and not just against my father. I was only two years old, and my older brother was six and was taking lessons from Dad. Tommy used to steal my food and pinch me, just to make me cry. He also bullied three-year-old Diane, telling her she was fat, even though there wasn't an ounce on her. Tracey was four and the winger at the time. She picked fights, beat us up and battered me regularly, but at least she made me laugh from time to time.

Things picked up after Mum left my father. She made a brave move and walked out on him, taking us four children with her. Our family and friends were relieved. We went straight round to Gran and Granddad's house and stayed there for a couple of nights while Mum got on to the council to find us another house.

Looking back on it now, I realize how incredibly strong my mother was to leave him, especially back then. She put us kids first, and took us out of a dangerous situation. It was a massive decision, and she knew some people would scorn her for leaving her husband and taking the four kids with her. Her strength and courage amaze me to this day. She set an example for us all: it was time for us to take control of our lives, too.

The council soon found us somewhere to live temporarily, about a block from our old house in Marion Square. We were there for two months, and then moved to Skelmersdale, an old coal-mining village on the outskirts of Liverpool, where the council houses served Liverpool's population, overflowing in the 1960s. Although we had no idea at the time, life was about to change dramatically.

With my father out of our lives, my mother's mood brightened considerably. I always thought she was the most beautiful woman in the world, with her flowing blonde hair and curvy figure. Her nickname was 'the Blonde Bombshell from Bootle'. Her sense of style was stunning, and she always dressed in the sexy fashions of the decade. She definitely turned heads on the streets of Skelmersdale.

She also caught the eye of her friend Pat's window cleaner, a man called John Bolster. Bolster was a bachelor who worked at the docks. He ran the window-cleaning service on the side, with his mate Jerry. Mum hired John to clean her windows, and the flirting began through the windowpanes. And who could resist my beautiful mother? Mum and John began dating and, six months later, we had a new dad. Pat and Jerry hooked up, too, and eventually married.

The change in our lives when Mum and John got married was incredible. We were plucked out of our shabby, abusive life and plunked into a whopping new house and into the arms of a blissfully happy mother and a loving new father. I was only three years old at the time, and revelled in the affection. Tommy, Tracey, Diane and I were all pleased to become Bolsters, although our last name was never officially changed.

Our new house, 83 Brierfield on the Skelmersdale Estate, was enormous – there were five bedrooms, so we all had our own space. My parents bought it from the council and took great pride in making it cosy and beautiful. It was on a lovely residential street with a real family feel.

Dad's pride and joy was the titanic aquarium he built into the wall in the front room. It held 220 gallons of water, bigger than some tanks at the Sea Life centre in Blackpool. People passing by on the street would often stop and peer in at the colourful coral and neon marine fish darting among the rocks. Little did they know that those small fish lived in constant terror of the poisonous lion fish that Dad insisted share the tank with them.

To feed the ravenous lion fish, Dad sent me fishing for sticklebacks at the local pond. They were tiny, and the lion fish devoured them as if they were a real feast. I fashioned my fishing pole out of a wooden stick and dangled some string on one end with a hookful of worms attached. I loved going fishing, but I detested my sisters' new name for me, 'Stickleback Joe from Mexico'. They chanted that awful rhyme for years.

Although we were dead proud of the aquarium, we all loathed cleaning the bloody thing. We would stand over the gigantic tank with a garden hose and suck as hard as we could to siphon the salt water out of it. I'll never forget how disgusting it tasted.

Mum was obsessed with keeping our new home pristine. She shooed us outside after breakfast – unless we were grounded, that is, which meant a dreary day spent upstairs in our bedrooms. I was always happy to get out of the house, to escape the stink of Dettol. I still can't bear the smell of it.

I would play every day in the massive garden, my favourite part of our new home. Dad landscaped it and put in magnificent flowers, a rockery, amazing conifer trees and a weeping willow. The rose bushes burst with blooms in season and trimmed shrubs bordered the lawn.

I played alone in this glorious garden for hours, and it became my sanctuary. When I see it today, it seems small, but to my three-year-old self, the garden was colossal, a magical playland full of enchanting adventures. Playing there gave wings to my imagination, and I spent hours transported into my own little world, with the spiders, worms, ants, birds and all the other animals and insects you find in a garden. I trapped angry bees in jars and stared at them through their glass cage as they exhausted themselves trying to buzz their way out. Things like that would keep me entertained for hours.

It was in this garden, lying on the soft grass and staring at the sky, that I started to see a beam of light whenever I caught a glimpse of somebody. It was very fleeting at that age, but it would grow stronger and stronger.

One thing that didn't quite fit in our well-kept garden was an old rusting car that stood in the centre of the yard. Nobody knew why it was there or how it had got there, but I loved it. I would sit in it and pretend that I was driving to faraway lands that only I knew existed – or so I thought. I often had the sense that a man was sitting next to me, in the passenger seat, joining me on these exotic trips. I would meet up with him later, in a profound way, but, back then, I really didn't think anything of it and pretty much ignored my invisible passenger.

In the old car and the garden, time did not exist. I created my world, and it was the only place I wanted to be. Daytime meant I could be in the garden, and the only interruptions were meals and bedtime. I adored my idyllic existence at three years of age, but the idyll was not to last long. My life was about to change again, in a massive and frightening way.

The change began in humiliating fashion in late summer, 1970. I was almost four years old, but my mother insisted on taking me to my first day of infant school strapped into a bulky silver pram with gigantic wheels. I may have been young, but I still felt that this was just downright embarrassing. I screamed, squirmed and struggled to get out of the straps, wanting to walk to school like all the other children. But Mum ignored my protests and pushed the pram right up to the gate. Only then did she release me and lift me down. I soon stopped crying when she stuffed a two-pence piece into my hand.

'Swap this for a biscuit at break time,' she said. The coin felt like pure gold, and I remember thinking that school might not be so bad after all.

My first day at St Luke's Primary School went okay, even though I much preferred my garden haven. I met a girl named Christine, and we became firm friends. We remained friends throughout school, and still are to this day.

The highlight of my first school day was break time. The teacher gave me a carton of milk, and I bought the biscuits in the green wrapper, because they were the ones that really caught my attention. Drinking that milk was sheer heaven. I had never tasted anything so smooth and glorious. I was hooked, and break time became the high point of the school day.

As the first week went on, I came to love our teacher, Mrs Grant. She kept us interested by handing out special treats like cream cakes, and even fussed over us lads who tried to be tough. She lived in a little bungalow near Baxter's supermarket, about a mile from the school. During the six-week summer holiday, she invited us to her home so we wouldn't get bored or into trouble. We all grew to adore her.

It was during one story time with my teacher that I had my first psychic vision. All the children sat cross-legged in a circle of carpeted blocks. I loved leaning my back against the wall and listening to Mrs Grant read.

That day, she started to tell a story about a cow grazing in a field. All of a sudden, the scene sprang to life, and a full-sized cow chewing on grass materialized in the middle of the classroom. I was stunned and confused in equal measure by this magical apparition. It was in full colour, complete with the field and hills. It was so real, I felt I could reach out and actually touch the cow.

Was this another one of Mrs Grant's treats, something to keep us listening, enchanted? But none of the other children were reacting. Why weren't they laughing and clapping their hands at the real cow in our classroom? After a few seconds, I was so absorbed in this bizarre image that I began to laugh uproariously.

'Pay attention, Joseph,' my teacher said patiently.

Her voice startled me, and the cow disappeared instantly. My awareness returned abruptly to the circle of children. But then, as she carried on reading, more images appeared from nowhere right before me.

'The farmer's wife collected eggs from the chickens in the barn,' Mrs Grant read.

I saw the scene right in front of me. I found it impossible to hold in how I felt and burst out laughing again.

'Please, Joseph,' the teacher pleaded. She couldn't understand what I was finding so funny, and the other kids glared at me for interrupting the story. It was then I realized that they couldn't see these panoramas, which were so vivid to me.

Every day, during story time, I saw dogs chasing cats, sharks eating fish, the moon talking to the sun – all as bright as day. I began to pay close attention to what I was seeing: it was as if the images were reflecting back off a projection screen at me.

Over the following weeks and months, the images became more than just visual; I could hear the noises the characters within the images were making and, at times,

I felt that if I reached out, I could touch them. They were so real, three-dimensional and in dramatic colour. My teacher and classmates had no idea what I was experiencing as they listened to the stories about a blue fish, a smiling lion or a flying carpet. They only knew that my inappropriate laughter was distracting them.

'Joe, please be quiet.' I could tell my precious teacher was losing patience. She eventually banished me to the corner, trying to punish me by excluding me from the story. It didn't help, because I could still hear her reading, and the visions continued. Later, she moved me into the hallway, and I would spend every story time there.

I became notorious as the one in the class who spoiled everything. My reputation spread to other classes, and I was constantly being told off, which confused me. Why were they so mean to me? I was only responding to what I was experiencing. It was now clear to me that I was the only one who saw these visions, but it still scared me to be disciplined for something I was unable to control. With the constant reprimands and the hostility from the other children, I began to hate story time. In fact, I started to loathe everything about school. I thought everyone hated me, and I couldn't understand why.

I didn't tell anybody about my visions, and I felt frighteningly alone. To protect myself, I started to act tough. I pretended that I didn't care about anything just to cover up, to stop myself from collapsing in a heap, out of fear and frustration.

2

Despite our lovely home, life in the Skelmersdale Estate in the early 1970s was miserable. There wasn't enough money to go round, and many parents struggled financially, so kids often had to go without. With no interesting places to explore and little to occupy themselves with, the kids had to find their own ways to amuse themselves – and sneaking around where we weren't supposed to be, stealing, fighting and lying were commonplace.

I learned this the hard way at the age of four, when my mother sent me down to the shops for milk and bread. I headed over the blue bridge towards the Digmoor Parade, which was a row of shops, with a pub called the Mucky Duck on it too.

I was wandering along, wondering what sweets I would be able to buy with the change. Suddenly, a brick whirred past my head and landed with a resounding crash on the road beside me. It just missed my foot. Then I heard loud cackling. My heart hammered in my chest as I jerked my head to see who had thrown the brick. Three older scallies glared at me, like hungry dogs ready to attack.

'Eh, Bolster, come here,' one said.

I knew my safest option was to run home but, if I did that, Mum would be angry that I hadn't done the shopping. I decided to ignore them, but my heart was still thumping. Even though I sensed that it was dangerous, I carried on towards the shop.

'Eh, you from number eighty-three. Come here now, Bolster!' another boy shouted.

Even though I had been born in the area, the Liverpool accent had never sounded quite so menacing and aggressive before. Even when Mum was angry, she didn't sound so harsh. My heart now thundering like a drum, I sized up the distances between myself and the shop and myself and the thugs. I knew I needed to get a move on before they gave chase. Thank goodness, I made it to the shop before they pounced.

Inside, I ducked to safety behind a shelf of drinks. I was relieved when the scallies didn't come in. I found where the bread and milk were, then slowly circled and browsed the three aisles over and over again for twenty minutes, until the shopkeeper asked me to leave.

I scanned the street; the coast was clear. I walked as fast as I could to the blue bridge, praying that I would be safe, my eyes darting suspiciously around. There was nowhere to hide and the bags were too heavy for me to be able to run, but luck was with me, and I made it over the blue bridge, thankful to see my house across the square.

'Joeeeeey,' a loud, whiny voice shouted, and then I heard laughter. My heart sank. Not only did I hate the name Joey, but now I faced a different gang – of seven-year-olds.

'Jooo-eeey,' another lad wheedled.

They must have seen me wince, because now they all

joined in, chanting my name, along with a string of insults. They started to circle me, like vultures around dead meat. My cheeks blazed hot. My God! I was only four years old and I was up against a gang of hoodlums, all much bigger than me.

'You're a Bolster,' the ringleader said with a glint in his eye.

'Yeah. What about it?' was all I managed to squeak. I tried to walk off, but one of them shoved me from behind, the coward. I stumbled and they laughed. I felt tears sting my eyes and tried desperately to hold them back, at least until I was safely inside my house. I don't know where it came from, but I turned and said with all the bravado I could muster, 'Our Tommy will kick your heads in when he hears about this. Leave me alone!'

I can't describe the pride and relief I felt when this worked. The bullies backed off and let me walk home in peace – that is, until I opened our back gate. Then they started to throw stones and taunt me from a distance.

I realized I would have to learn to defend myself in my neighbourhood. I would have to toughen up to survive.

When I was five, two of my friends from infant school – Eddie Speakman and Steven Rutliege, or 'Ruttie' as we called him – who lived near by on the Skelmersdale Estate, often came to our house to play. One of our favourite adventures was egging. Lots of birds made their nests in the trees in our garden, and we'd search each nest and collect the prettiest eggs. Then we'd stick a pin in each end of the egg and blow the liquid out, rinse and dry them, and then put all the beautiful eggs, of various sizes and colours, on display.

One day, I found a blackbird's nest in a birch tree. Since my pals were not around, I took it down and found two chicks and three eggs inside. The chicks were so fragile that I felt instantly protective of them.

Suddenly, I heard a stern voice. 'Don't touch those birds. Their mum and dad won't know where to find their babies to feed them and keep them warm.' The voice sounded just as my own father's did when he was telling me not to do something, except this voice didn't belong to anybody. I also felt a strong presence there with me in the garden, and knew that was where the voice was coming from. It was the same essence, I was sure, that joined me on my adventures in the old car.

It frightened me a bit, but I was too excited about my find to be too scared. Afraid that the birds might be cold, I ignored the voice and sneaked the nest into the house. My hands were shaking for fear that my mother would catch me. The tiny birds squeaked loudly, and I could hear Mum and Dad in the front room. If they found out what I was doing, I knew they would make me put the nest back in the tree.

At that moment, two of my siblings banged into the house, making so much clatter that I was able to scurry past the front room and up the stairs. Safe in my room, I placed the nest and the squawking birds under my bed. They sounded as if they were hungry and, now, it was my duty to provide them with food. I ran out to the garden, and hunted down three scrawny worms.

I named my little birds Woody and Bonzo and put the wiggly worms into the nest. Woody and Bonzo went wild and screeched so loudly I was certain my parents would hear. Instead, my sister Diane entered the room and sucked in a huge breath when she saw them.

'I'm going to tell Mum and Dad,' she taunted.

I hurriedly pulled a ten-pence piece from my pocket and shoved it at her, warning her not to tell. Then I put the nest back in the tree.

The next morning, I rushed out to the birch tree to check on my little chicks. To my horror, they were dead. I was struck by a profound sense of loss, a hollow emptiness pervading my chest. I thought of the voice that had warned me not to take the nest. If I had listened to it, the baby birds would still be alive. I felt crushed with guilt.

I cried and, instinctively, I knew I had to apologize and say goodbye to the little chicks. I wrapped the tiny bodies in toilet paper and buried them under a rock in the garden. I held a little service and said I was extremely sorry for their pain and death. It was my first encounter with death and grief, and the sense of devastation and guilt lingered for years.

I remember all the memories coming back with full force one time when I was waiting for the school bus at the age of ten or eleven. I saw a cat dive for a bird and gulp it into its mouth. I chased the cat and wrenched its mouth open to retrieve its prey but, of course, that bird, too, was dead.

Although Eddie, Ruttie and I continued to go egging

for many years after that, it was only to discover eggs. I never again touched another nest nor allowed Eddie or Ruttie to disturb one.

Soon after this introduction to grief and loss, I was plunged into it on a much deeper level. When I was five, my dad was diagnosed with a stomach ulcer and went into hospital to have it treated. The doctors sliced him open for the routine operation but, unfortunately, infection set in soon after the surgery. His stomach swelled and he was in and out of the operating theatre for a week. Dad ended up on life support.

He did come home, finally, but his stomach was never the same after that. I can remember him lying in bed, a bowl next to him to catch the putrid green bile he was retching up. As a child, it was difficult to watch my once-hearty dad in such misery.

He was in hospital on a regular basis for years and years and had eight to ten more major operations for the same problem. He tried hard to keep working, but he was so sick his boss sent him home most days. In the end, he had to give up his job.

It was a traumatic time for all of us. By then, the family had expanded, with the arrival of my half-brothers, Johnny and Denny. It would eventually inflate to ten children in all, with the addition of Maria, Heidi, Louise and Peter.

During the early years of Dad's illness, I would slip into my bed and bury myself in my blankets to muffle my crying. I didn't want to upset Mum, who had enough on her hands keeping our huge family functioning. Watching Dad so ill and being constantly afraid that he would die shook me to the core, and particularly when he was in hospital.

At this time, when I was still very young, an amazing man visited me in a dream. His image is still crystal clear in my mind: he was a stocky man with a jovial sense of humour. He introduced himself as my mum's Uncle Tom, which made him my great-uncle. It turned out to be my formal introduction to the presence that had been with me in the old car and the voice that had warned me about the baby birds.

'Your dad will be okay, Joe,' my kindly great-uncle reassured me.

I totally believed him, and was very relieved and excited when I woke up the next morning. I told my mum about the dream, but she dismissed it and told me to run along. I tried to tell her again later that day, but she shooed me away again.

After that, I figured that the vision in my dream must have been just that, and that I couldn't trust in it, so I started worrying about my dad again. It upset me more than being punished and made fun of at school, more than being bullied on the estate.

Mum visited Dad every day when he was in hospital, and we kids were often shipped off to Auntie Nora's house until he came home. Mum was the eldest of eleven children, and Nora was one of her middle sisters. She lived in a fancy house with swanky furnishings. She and

Uncle Ken enjoyed a certain lifestyle and had three perfect children to go with it.

Auntie Nora must have cringed when we Bolster kids bounded into her elegant house like un-housetrained puppies. She confined us to a few rooms and expected us to sit quietly and be polite, like her kids were. It just wasn't me, and I would dissolve into tantrums, throwing myself on the floor, kicking and screaming.

'I want my mummy!' I wailed. 'Where's my mummy?'

Auntie Nora didn't know whether to wallop me or give me a hug.

I did get on with their youngest daughter, Gillian. I remember that when she visited us in Skelmersdale she was amazed by Dad's massive fish tank. I was in my element pointing out everything to Gillian, and I let her feed the fish. One day, watching her sprinkle the tank with food, I had a sudden intuition. She just didn't look healthy, and I knew instinctively that something bad was going to happen to her. It frightened me, because I was really fond of her.

Shortly afterwards, Gillian died of leukemia. She was seven. We were all grief-stricken. I didn't tell anybody that I had been forewarned about what was going to happen to her. I was so sad about her dying and really wanted to tell someone about the omen I had experienced. I couldn't, of course and, again, I felt really alone and frightened.

Soon after Gillian's death, I had a vivid dream. I was sweating from a blast of extreme heat. Suddenly, I saw Dad at a funeral. There were two coffins, and other mourners were crowding around them. I woke up sweltering but shivering in fear. Once again, I told nobody.

A little while later, my cousins John and Paul were driving back from London, having been there to watch a football match. They crashed the car and it burst into flames. Both boys died. After this happened, Auntie Nora began wearily to tolerate my tantrums, having come to understand my terror that Dad could die.

With my dad ill and our house in chaos, I started hanging round more with my mates, Eddie and Ruttie. I was used to my muddled home life and considered it normal. I didn't realize what I was missing until I started spending time at Eddie's house. I noticed that his mother showered him with love and attention. He wiped her kisses off his cheeks, but I really wanted attention like that. I felt really envious when I saw Eddie receiving all that affection, something I didn't get in my own hectic home.

My poor mother was saddled with the weight of all her children, a sick husband and having to do a mountain of chores as well as going to work. She just didn't have time to read us bedtime stories like Eddie's mum did her children. We never got to sit in her lap for cuddles, and she never handed out random hugs or kisses.

My dad tried, too, but really he wasn't much better. When Mum was in hospital having her babies, he would make us bread and butter pudding, even though he was sick. It tasted like mush, but we all said it was delicious. It felt good that he was trying to give us a treat.

My parents had to be strict, because they just didn't

have the capacity to handle any additional problems such as unruly children. There were no lovey-dovey moments or shows of affection from Mum or Dad, so we learned not to mess with them. That was just how it was. Any infraction was immediately punished with three days' confinement to our bedrooms.

I don't blame my parents for not having enough time to give me during my childhood. I know they did the best they could under difficult circumstances and provided us with the basics, such as food, clothing and warm shelter. I was jealous of Eddie, but his loving home life gave me a glimpse into what kindness and affection could be. It showed me another way of life and gave me hope.

Meanwhile, my own life over the next few years continued with the same complications. For example, every time I went to the butcher's to fetch meat for Mum, I saw flashes of a coffin around the butcher. It frightened me, and I tried to shake the visions away, but they persisted. The butcher committed suicide some time later. I can't even begin to explain how terrifying these death premonitions were. I was still only a young lad, after all.

When I was seven, my family was scraping by on Mum's measly salary from her job at the local chippie. My brothers, sisters and I loved Mum's job, because she often brought home huge bags of chips after work. With Dad not working, she barely made ends meet. Out of her meagre wages, she did manage to give each of us kids ten pence a week pocket money. But even though this was generous given our dire financial situation, it was never enough for me. I don't know what it was, but something within me drove me to do things that I knew were bad at the time and, today, make me even more ashamed.

I stole my Mum's precious savings. I knew she kept them under a pastel-coloured statue of Our Lady on a shelf above her bed. My parents' bedroom was off limits to the children, a virtually sacred space we dared not invade. I knew I was taking a risk by sneaking into the bedroom, but I did it anyway.

I remember hearing the sound of my heart pounding in my ears and my hands shaking as I leaned over the bed, not daring to wrinkle the covers, and lifted up the statue. There was a ten-pound note! I caught my breath. Imagine how much chocolate I could buy with that.

But as I reached for the money, I heard a woman's voice. 'Don't touch that!' she said sternly. It was not my mother or either of my sisters; it came from my inner ear. I heard these voices from time to time and usually ignored them, convincing myself that what they said didn't matter because I couldn't see who was speaking.

I ignored it this time too. I snatched the money, a real fortune in those days, scurried out of the room and ran straight to the shops. I bought a Mars bar from a man who sold things from his van, 'the Mobile Shop', and forced myself to save it until I got back home. I stole out to the garden and sank into the grass. I ripped the wrapper from the chocolate bar and drooled over every delectable bite. While it lasted, it was worth all the stress of getting it.

The moment the final sweetness melted from my

mouth I realized I had a new problem. I now possessed nine pound notes and a handful of coins. Mum would know she had left a ten-pound note under the statue; returning the change would only incriminate me. I had to dispose of the evidence, and fast. I found a soft patch of soil by the fence that ran along the back garden. I dug a hole, stuffed the money into it and covered it over. To my seven-year-old mind, I was home free.

The next morning I heard my mother shouting. 'You kids get in here now!' she yelled.

It was then, I'm embarrassed to say, that the guilt hit; to my shame, it was overwhelmed by a sense of panic.

We all congregated in the front room. Mum was livid. She paced back and forth, her eyes assaulting us with suspicious looks. I tried my best to look relaxed.

'There was a ten-pound note in my bedroom, and this morning it isn't bloody there. I know one of you took it! Which one of you did it?' she demanded, looking from one terrified child to the next.

I decided right then and there that I could not confess.

She carried on pacing. 'Who took it?' she insisted, her voice growing louder. 'Someone must have pinched it, because it was there yesterday and it's gone today. Who stole the money?'

Nobody spoke up, and she went ballistic. She screamed like a madwoman. 'Who took the bloody money from my room?' Then, realizing that if she carried on like this, the neighbours would soon come knocking, she switched strategies.

'If whoever did it owns up, I will not tell your father,' she coaxed.

I didn't trust Mum; I knew she would tell Dad anyway. And I knew he would spank me across the hand with a leather belt when he found out. I stepped forward. I knew even then that what I was doing was unforgivable. In a small voice I said, 'I know who took the money.'

All eyes were on me as I danced from foot to foot. 'It was our Tracey, Mum. I saw her take the money and go down to the shops to buy chocolate. Then she hid the rest of the money outside.'

I chose Tracey because she wasn't in the room at the time. I thought Mum would cool down once she had an answer, but she flew out of the room, shouting for my sister. My guilt and shame grew legs and started kicking me violently in the stomach. I heard Tracey wailing and sobbing loudly. I hurried to the kitchen.

'He's lying, Mum! It wasn't me,' she cried. 'Tell her the truth, Joe.'

I couldn't do it. I was too much of a coward. 'Just admit it, Tracey,' I said.

My poor sister could do nothing but endure the spanking that should have been mine. I could only look on. I felt terrible. Mum was furious and Tracey would never forgive me. What had I done?

By the time I was halfway through my time at St Luke's Junior School, I was considered a lost cause. I had a real reputation as a disruptive troublemaker. The moment I walked into a classroom, the teachers and children would be on their guard. I was never able to relax at school, and maybe that is why I had more and more visions, and they became ever more vivid.

When I was eight, I had a teacher called Miss Simmonds, who I thought was really cruel. To me, she seemed – at the age of forty – like a dinosaur. She didn't care at all about the children. In those days, Catholic schools in Britain could be scary places. Miss Simmonds was a tyrant, and she slammed the fear of God into all of us. She followed a 1950s regime of discipline and nobody dared to take liberties with her. She would give anyone who got out of line in class a clip round the ear and drag them to the headmaster's office. And it was as if Mr Bartholomew had some kind of a pact with her, because he was just as brutal. You knew you were in for a tough punishment if you wound up in his office.

Miss Simmonds enjoyed shouting and giving out evil stares, and she would decide on a whim that a student deserved a grilling in front of the class. She would grab the kid by the wrist, leaving painful nail marks, and would clobber children over the head with school books. She thought children were inherently naughty and she delighted in punishing them. I was a permanent target.

As you can imagine, by that point I hated school. I was having trouble concentrating because my visions were growing stronger and more bizarre. I would give in to them and slip inside my mind, watching each fresh page of images that was laid out before me.

One day, I started to feel drowsy and disorientated during a lesson. I had never felt like that before so I panicked, but the feeling also provided a distraction from the boring class, so eventually I relaxed and gave myself up to it. I felt my consciousness separate in a sort of whoosh. Suddenly, I was no longer at school sitting at my desk; I was somehow out of my body. I was light and floating above an ambulance, trying to peer inside. In the vehicle, an elderly man lay motionless on a stretcher.

'Come on, stay with me,' a paramedic urged desperately.

The old man did not move.

'We're losing him,' said another paramedic. 'He's going.'

'No! Stay with me.'

'He's dying. He's going.'

The medics tried frantically to revive the old man. I saw the old man separate from himself. I was stunned. Now I could see two versions of him. The first, which the paramedics were still working on, looked dense and sickly, with rubbery skin. The second looked light, healthy and full of vitality and was smiling broadly.

'He's dead,' said the first paramedic.

I couldn't believe it. I shouted out that the man was not dead but very much alive and well. In fact, he was standing right next to me and smiling! I tried to attract their attention, but they could neither see nor hear me. Then I was rudely snatched away from the scene and snapped back into my body in the classroom. I felt disorientated again. My vision was blurred and my mind was foggy. I was confused about where I was, but I felt fingernails digging into my wrist. My witchy teacher dragged me from my desk to the front of the class, whacking my back, which snapped me even further to attention.

'Joseph Bolster! Please share with the class exactly what you were thinking and, more importantly, the lesson I am trying to teach,' she droned sarcastically.

I heard snickering from a couple of lads at the back of the classroom. The rest of the class looked terrified. I decided not to say a word and put up with the slaps on my wrist with a ruler.

Later, I learned that I had been muttering while I was away on my ambulance adventure and had actually shouted out loud exactly what I said to the paramedics. No wonder Miss Simmonds and the class were alarmed. They had no idea that my mind had not been in my body when it happened. That was my first out-of-body experience (OBE).

I only got a few days' break before my next one. This time, I found myself in a house in which the son had overdosed on drugs. The paramedics were trying to resuscitate him on the living-room floor while his horrified parents looked on helplessly. Just as with the man in the ambulance, I instantly and intuitively knew information about these people and their lives.

'He's dead, isn't he?' his mother wailed. 'My boy is dead!' She sobbed on her husband's shoulder.

The teenager on the carpet looked pale and sick, sweat beading on his forehead. Then I saw a second version of him, with full colour in his face, infused with vigour and happiness. Why were his parents so upset and proclaiming him dead when I could clearly see him standing right there in front of them looking perfectly healthy?

After this OBE, I wound up in the headmaster's office, where he whipped my hand with a leather strap. Despite my efforts not to react to the pain, I winced. But I also felt a presence around me offering me strength. I didn't understand this *charisma* which moved in during these times of strife then, but I was certainly grateful for it.

3

The OBEs were now coming two to three times a week. I still saw the happy, healthy versions of people separating from their physical bodies. Many times I travelled to vast, open spaces in the countryside and floated over meadows, hills and sometimes farms. I would see farmers bouncing along on tractors as they ploughed the fields, cows grazing lazily on the hills, chickens pecking dried rice from the ground and farmhands working the land.

I began to look forward to the OBEs which took me to visit these places, which were so different to what I knew. I'd barely been out of Skelmersdale and had never seen a farm, so I was fascinated by them and longed to go to one in person. I often strolled down the hill on our estate trying to spot one of the farms in the distance, hoping to visit so that I could physically experience what I saw in the OBEs.

I wanted to ask someone where I might actually find a farm, but a strong internal radar told me that they would just think I was mad, especially the lads I hung out with, so I kept it to myself, and the teachers went on disciplining me, not knowing that I was having these experiences which I could not control.

As I'd never been far from home, you can imagine my excitement when my class went on a field trip to

Edinburgh. At £2.50, the ticket was a stretch for my parents but, in the event, the fare was refunded because the train was overbooked and we had to stand for the three-and-a-half-hour journey. I was overjoyed to be going on a trip out of my small neighbourhood. Edinburgh Castle, an ancient fortress on the top of a stone mountain called Castle Rock, was fantastic; I had never seen anything quite so majestic. The first thing I saw when I entered the grounds was a lovely woman in her twenties carrying a basket of fruit and smiling at me. I nudged my mate.

'Look at that woman. Isn't she lovely?'

'What woman?'

'The lady standing over there in the long red dress holding a basket.'

My friend squinted in that direction. 'I don't see anybody, Joe.'

I didn't take any notice of what he said because the woman's smile radiated warmth and filled me with a wonderful feeling. Within seconds, she had disappeared.

'Where did that lady go?' I asked my teacher. I took off in the direction of the castle, trying to find her, but was quickly rounded up and brought back to where the rest of the class was standing. I was sad that the woman had gone. The feeling of warmth I'd had from her melted away as I walked further into the castle grounds with my classmates, to be replaced with a sickly feeling in the pit of my stomach as we entered the castle.

What I saw next revolted me to the core. In a flash

vision that lasted only seconds I saw a man's body dressed in shabby brown clothing. And, next to him, on the floor, lay his head!

Then another image flashed before me, of a fat man lying dead on the ground. Other, similar scenes flickered before my eyes. It was as if I were watching a horror movie on television. I panicked and screamed, which once again upset the teacher. I wished I could tell her about the frightening movie clips in my head and ask her to explain to me what they were but, as usual, I was alone.

My terror subsided as we were eating our lunch outside. The other kids teased me about my appalling display in the castle, but I ignored them. Instead, I gazed at the woman in red, who had now reappeared.

'There she is!' I shouted, hoping everyone would see her and that I would be vindicated. I saw her mouth move, but I couldn't hear a voice.

Instead I read her lips: 'The others can't see me.'

Why was I the only one who could see the pretty woman? I would have given anything for there to be someone who could help me understand the strange things that were happening to me.

The class outing to the castle really was quite a trip. On the tour, we learned that human habitation of the land it occupies dates back to the ninth century BC, although most of the current structure dates from the sixteenth century. No wonder the grounds were so spiritually active. The castle has always been a military garrison and is still used for military administration today.

I know many people died violent deaths there ... because I saw them.

School continued to be a source of upset and confusion. Church was challenging, too. I was raised a Catholic but I never had the remotest interest in organized religion. Every Sunday morning was torture, with my parents pulling me out of bed or away from the television to attend mass. I was always bored and resentful and never paid any attention to the priest.

One tedious Sunday, I watched an elderly woman shuffle to the front of the church and drop a shiny fifty-pence piece into the collection box, then dip her hand back in to collect change. An idea took root in my mind. I felt in my pocket for my weekly ten-pence piece. I took it out, hid it in my hand and motioned my younger brother Johnny to follow me to the front of the church.

I plunged the coin into the collection box, then scooped my hand back in and counted out three ten-pence pieces, pretending it was change for fifty pence. Then I stepped aside for Johnny to do the same thing, because he had quickly picked up on what I had done.

'Put that back!' a stern female voice in my head commanded.

I froze in my tracks. This was the same voice that had told me not to steal my mother's money. Whoever she was, she definitely grabbed my attention, and I made my way back to the pew feeling extremely guilty that I had stolen money from the church and encouraged my little brother to do the same. However, back then, I was young, and I didn't feel guilty for long. My remorse soon vanished when I thought of the sweets I could buy with the money.

I was excited and restless throughout the rest of the service and, when it ended, Johnny and I flew to the shop across the road and spent the money on sweets. I was thrilled because they stocked liquorice, my favourite. After that we did it every week – never too much, just enough for our treats.

And our thieving didn't stop there. There was a bloke I knew called John Mealaw, who was married, with kids. He drove a taxi, which he called Ringo, after Ringo Starr, and he made a tidy living at it. His big mistake was to leave Ringo unlocked overnight. I sneaked into the taxi and skimmed his nightly takings. This went on for months, until he caught on and hid, waiting to catch the thief.

Sure enough, he caught me and turned me in to my parents. They gave me a real hiding, but even that didn't put me off. I was only eight, but I knew I wanted money. I'm not proud of it now but, despite the disembodied woman's warning and my parents' wrath, I continued to steal money any way I could.

That same year, I was sitting in class waiting for one of my visions or OBEs, something to take me out of the tedium of school. At that time, my visions were frequent, but they didn't really have anything to do with my own life. I simply went along for the ride and enjoyed the view.

But, on this day, as I drifted into my daydream, a vision showed me a boy hanging out of a window. When I looked closely I realized it was a lad called David from our school. The scene unnerved me because, in my vision, David was in danger. This was too close to home. Up until now, it had been easy to detach myself from the deaths I witnessed via OBEs, because I didn't know the people.

Flashes of this vision of David hanging from a window ledge continued for a few days and they freaked me out. I knew David was in serious trouble, but I didn't know what to do about it. I still hadn't told anyone about my visions, and I didn't dare share this one with anyone either.

A few days later, I was walking out of the gates when I heard sirens wailing, coming closer and closer to the school. I noticed that there was a crowd gathering.

'Hang on, boy!' a man shouted.

I looked up and saw David dangling out of a window, his legs flapping against the brick wall below. I was shocked. This was exactly what I had seen in my vision. I stepped back from the crowd and thought about it.

I suddenly realized the truth about the OBEs and visions. The healthy versions of the people that separated from the ill ones were very much alive. I had never understood why the families were crying and saying they were dead. To me, the fact that they were healthy seemed something to celebrate, not mourn. The separated entities were peaceful and content, so I had never been frightened of them. But, at that moment, I understood that I had been witnessing actual death scenes. Did this mean that David was about to die, too?

In my vision of David, I didn't see him die, but this

real-life playback was too frightening for me. I hurried home in a daze, again not saying a word to anyone. I heard the next day that David had been rescued. What a relief *that* was!

About a year later, when I was nine, Dad fell ill again and an ambulance came to rush him to hospital. My family was frantic at the thought of losing him. One day I went with Mum to visit him.

The journey to the hospital was quite an adventure, and we hopped on and off several buses amidst all the hustle and bustle of Liverpool. As I said, I didn't spend much time outside our estate, so all the noise, people and sights were dead exciting to me. I couldn't wait to get home and tell my brothers and sisters about it.

My mother sat silently beside me. I looked over at her and realized that her youthful beauty had faded. She looked worn down and pale, a shadow of her former self. Her appearance upset me, but I told myself it was because of the stress about Dad's condition and turned my attention to looking out of the window of the bus.

Once we arrived at Broadgreen Hospital, my excitement drained away. The moment I stepped through the revolving door, an image flashed through my mind: row upon row of heavy black army boots were neatly lined up, and there were grey-green camouflage uniforms scattered about. I had the sensation that there were soldiers there, but I couldn't see any. The image went beyond walls and space, and I knew I was the only one seeing all this military paraphernalia.

I said nothing to my mother as we walked along the corridor to Dad's ward. Standing outside his door, my stomach lurched, and I was instantly overwhelmed with fear and panic. The hospital felt dirty somehow. The place looked and smelled sterile, but I had a strong sensation of deep-seated filth which could not be cleaned away. It felt like death, and I found it seriously disturbing.

The moment I stepped into Dad's room, I saw a sight that none of my other visions had prepared me for. A man with flowing white hair and a fluttering gown floated over a patient a few beds down from Dad. This ghostlike entity was stunningly clear and was staring straight at me. All at once, I knew the man in the bed was going to die. This was different from the OBEs I had experienced in the classroom; I was seeing this floating person in my real life. I let out a gasp.

'Are you all right, son?' Dad asked.

I pulled my gaze away to look at my father. He seemed fragile, hooked up to wires and tubes, and I fought the urge to cry. Knowing the man a few beds down was going to die soon made me all the more worried about my dad.

'How are you feelin', Dad?' I asked.

He shrugged his scrawny shoulders. 'How are the fish doin' at home?'

'They're still alive,' I said. I sneaked a glance above the other man's bed and, sure enough, the hovering ghost was still there. I had a feeling it was waiting to greet the man when he died.

I didn't find the return journey on the bus as exciting

as the journey out. I was relieved to be home again, where I was familiar with the space and the visions I saw. The image of the ghost stuck with me for months. Once again, I didn't tell anyone about it. And neither did I say a word about the visions that were to follow.

Up until the time I saw the floating ghost, I had sensed presences, heard voices, seen images and visited places in my mind. The experiences grew stronger after infant school, and more vivid and bizarre. Sometimes I felt over-whelmed, but I usually managed to handle it all, and faced the consequences if I disturbed other people. At least then they wouldn't think I was acting up because I was totally mad.

After the floating-ghost incident, however, things got a bit spooky. Suddenly, there were spirits following me everywhere. I could handle the scary guy in the tattered, brown jacket who hung around me as I walked with mates from school. It was easy to ignore spirits like that one, because there were people around to distract me. I knew my mates couldn't see the ghost, so I pretended not to notice him either.

The worst part was at home. I saw spirits everywhere – in the kitchen, in the living room, in my bedroom, every-where! They looked just like other human beings with dense bodies, but they would appear and disappear in an instant. That was how I could tell they weren't of this earth. They never said anything to me, but I was somehow imbued with a sense of who they were, their personalities and what they were about. However, the information meant nothing to me, because I didn't know these people in my real life. They scared me to death!

I started to dread going home. I was so frightened I finally decided I had to tell my brothers and sisters, in order not to have to suffer alone.

I shared a small bedroom with Johnny and Denny. We had a bunk bed, and I slept on the top while my brothers shared the bottom. I was glad to have them so close to me at night when the spirits invaded the space. I was absolutely terrified of these dead people. I was only nine years old, and I was dealing with all this crazy stuff on my own. One night, I was trying to fall asleep but, as usual, the spirits gathered. I leaned over the side of the bed and looked at Denny and Johnny, who were snoring lightly, tucked up tightly next to each other. I felt so envious that they were sleeping, without a care in the world. I crept out of bed and shook Denny awake.

'Hey,' I whispered in his ear, and then quickly hopped back on to the top bunk. 'Do you know that there's a woman standing right next to you?'

'Where?' He scrambled on to his elbows and looked around the room.

'Right there next to you. She was watching you while you slept.'

Denny's eyes widened. Finally, someone else was feeling what I experienced all the time.

'She has blonde hair and creepy blue eyes.'

'You're lying!' Denny was fighting back tears.

'No, she's really there, and she's a ghost. You can't see her, but she can see you.'

Little did Denny know that this spirit woman often visited our bedroom and would stand next to the bed, reeking of cigarettes.

'Shut up, Joe, or I'll tell Mum on you!'

'Mum can't stop her. She's chopping off her hair right now and putting it on your head. She's reaching out for you!' I knew what I was doing was mean, but I was so desperate to share what I was experiencing and no longer have to go through it all alone.

Denny's shrill scream cut through the house and jolted Johnny out of his sleep. Denny flew out of the room, and soon returned with Mum. She gave me a serious bollocking for scaring the younger kids and asked me why I wasn't asleep. That was the first time I was tempted to tell her, but I didn't. I sensed she would neither understand nor believe me, and that would be worse than being told off for frightening my brothers.

Sharing my fright with Denny eased my burden a bit, so I went on telling him about the ghosts in the room. I knew it was wrong to scare him, but I just couldn't stand being alone with my fears any longer. I told my other brothers and sisters, too, during the day.

They accused me of making it all up, but I caught them looking around the room when I entered. They were afraid. Telling them was selfish, but it did help me to share my terrors, although I never told anyone the whole truth.

With the last day of school term approaching, I sat in class and daydreamed about the luscious six weeks off to come – nothing but lazy days with my mates. I couldn't wait to escape the dreariness of school.

On the first day of the summer holidays, Mum assigned me to look after our Denny, who was six years old at the time. While we were playing outside, Denny noticed a dead blackbird. He started to prod and poke at the thing. My fondness for birds kicked in and I shouted, 'Leave that bird alone!'

Denny ignored me, scooped up the limp bird and ran off down the street with it.

I chased after him and watched in utter shock as he hurled the wilted bird through our neighbours' open window.

The house belonged to an Indian couple. We didn't really know them, because they kept themselves to themselves but, after the bird soared through that window, there was a boisterous scream from the man, and it scared us into running away. We ran as if the hounds of hell were after us.

Safe in our house, we thought the incident was over, until the couple banged and screamed at the back door. Mum and Dad ran to see what the commotion was. Denny hid behind a chair, peeking his head out like a mouse.

'Your son threw a blackbird into our house!' the man bellowed. 'In our culture, a dead bird in the house is a bad omen and means death.'

Those words burned into my mind.

'He has brought bad fortune to my family.' The man yelled and cursed at Denny, who was still behind the chair.

Mum finally calmed the man, and kept Denny inside with her the rest of the day. But I would never forget that a dead bird in the house meant death.

That same year, my big brother Tommy turned punk and dyed his hair bright red and yellow. He and his teenage mates hung out at a tree house they had built at the bottom of our road. I liked hanging out with the big boys, who always seemed to be up to something cool. They dressed in tight, skinny jeans, black T-shirts with images like skulls and swords on them, chains, leather jackets, boots and, sometimes, hats, and wore their hair spiky and in outrageous arrays of colours, from hot-pink to grass-green.

The parents on the estate were afraid of the growing punk culture back then. Tommy and his pals ran away to the tree house to escape Mum and Dad's negative opinion of them. One time, Tommy stayed in the tree house for a whole week. Mum sent me down to fetch him, and I enjoyed being there with his mates.

That summer, Tommy and his mates organized a camping trip. Staying up late, hunting and hanging out sounded as if it would be a real adventure. I wanted so badly to go, but I was afraid to ask Tommy. Instead, I asked Dad for permission to join them.

'Tommy told me I had to ask you,' I lied. I looked so eager that Dad said yes and let me go.

Unfortunately, Tommy and his mates had already left on the trip, and I didn't know what direction they had gone in. Tommy had told me they were going to

Rainford, which was only a few miles up the road, so I headed out that way, excited about finding them and joining in the fun with Tommy and his best mates, Mooey and Cliffy.

With their neon hair, they should have been easy to find, but even though I walked for what seemed like miles, I didn't find them. I felt lost and asked a few people if they had seen a group of punks passing by. Nobody had.

Somewhere near St Helens, I started to trudge along a countryside track, tired and hungry. It was getting dark and I was frightened, as there was no sign of my brother and his friends. I continued walking along the deserted road, surrounded by old trees, the noises of night and dark silhouettes that, to a nine-year-old, looked evil. I suddenly realized that my brother thought I was at home, and everyone at home thought I was with Tommy. If something happened to me, nobody would know. I was totally alone, and the fear seeped slowly in.

I tried to think of other times when I'd been in a sticky situation and things had come out all right, like the time when Tommy pushed me under the railings of a horse pen. I screamed for my life when he dropped hay on me, and we both laughed when a horse ate it off my head.

But thinking about the scrapes I had been in before did nothing to assuage my fear about my current predicament. This was life or death.

Panic took the place of rational thinking, and I screamed out loud. 'Tommy!' I began to shout. Maybe someone will remember hearing my cries after the police find my body, I thought. I yelled Tommy's name over and over, but the silence swallowed my words. I was utterly alone – or so I thought.

I stumbled numbly in the darkness and somehow ended up inside a graveyard. The moon scattered a faint light among the headstones, and my mind started to play tricks on me. The gravestones seemed to be popping up from out of the ground, then a church outside the cemetery loomed close, then zoomed back into place.

The total silence exaggerated the sound of my heart throbbing in my ears, and the stillness allowed me to feel every drop of blood pumping through my veins. Tall, spiky, sinister railings stabbed skyward around the edge of the graveyard. It was as if they were holding me hostage, and I couldn't find an opening to escape.

That's when the voices started. Far away and subtle at first, they grew louder and more direct. I heard chattering and laughing, as if there were a garden party going on. Everything at the party seemed normal and jovial. I didn't see anyone, but I clearly heard them. It was like walking about with my eyes closed, listening to people all around me talking. I was terrified that I would see these people in the same way I saw the spirits in my house and at school. I didn't want to see them here, in this frightening graveyard, while I was all alone.

I turned and ran back in the direction I had come, feeling as though I was being chased by disembodied voices, which grew louder and louder the faster I tried to escape them. I searched and searched for a way out of this dreadful cemetery.

A misty cloud blocked out the moon, trapping me in

darkness. I ran my hands along the gothic railings, trying to find a space between them, or a loose or broken one. I screamed and cried, not caring who heard me. I needed someone to rescue me, and I didn't care who – police officer, priest or down-and-out.

The voices continued to torment me as I followed the fence round. Finally, I decided that the only way out was to jump over the tall, dagger-like railings. I didn't care if I hurt myself. I climbed quickly, adrenaline fuelling my strength and speed. I swung myself over the spikes without catching anything but my shirt, which ripped on the way down the other side.

I ran and ran in the direction I thought I had come from. I felt that, since I had survived the evil graveyard, I could endure anything. I was on autopilot, sweating from the exertion but shivering from cold and shock. I saw a flurry of lights in the distance. I realized they were coming from shops and houses. As I drew closer, I also heard the voices of real people I could see. I recognized the shops and found my way home from there. Never had I felt so relieved and grateful to be home.

To this day, I don't know how I made it home that night. Did someone or something lead me back to safety? Why was I experiencing these visions and voices? As far as I knew, nobody else did.

By the time I was ten years old, I had started to question who I was and what my purpose was in this world. Why was I here?

Every so often, I had an odd flash of the spirit world as

it existed before I was born. One spirit teacher told me I was on earth to find knowledge. That was confusing. Most of the time, I felt I was walking around with a restless emptiness inside me that I did not understand. Why did nobody else see the spirits or visions, hear the voices or soar out of their body like I did? These strange encounters were getting me nowhere, and they certainly weren't providing me, or anyone else, with any real knowledge. Even in a room full of people, I usually felt alone.

Despite being confused and frightened on one level – or perhaps to seek some kind of compensation for it – I became totally preoccupied with money. I did a paper round at that time, but the pay was never enough. Teachers and my parents drummed into me that the love of money is the root of all evil, but the temptation to beg, borrow and steal it took over my entire life.

That summer, I was dying to join my mates Eddie and Ruttie down at the swimming baths. I had already spent my wages and my week's pocket money, and had nothing left to go swimming with. I was in the garden trying to figure out how to get my hands on some cash when I heard my mother calling me.

'I need you to go down to the shops and get me some bacon and coffee,' she said, handing me some money.

It felt great to have the money in my hands. On my way to the shops, I decided to nick the bacon and coffee and use Mum's money to get into the swimming baths. And I would have enough left over to buy myself a curry on the way home.

I chose the Co-op because I knew it would be busy which I thought would make it less likely that anybody would notice me stealing. I walked down the aisle to the refrigerated section and looked around to see if anybody was watching me. I nabbed the bacon and stuffed it down the front of my tracksuit bottoms – the elastic waistband made things very easy. I found the coffee and slipped it into my shirtsleeve. I looked about again and was certain as I made my way to the exit that nobody had seen me steal the goods. My heart was hammering in my chest as I approached the barriers. I was so close to success – then, all of a sudden, somebody jumped on me.

My fright soared to panic and I started to wrestle with them. I quickly realized it was an old woman. She had evidently seen me stealing the food and was now all over me, yanking my hair and screaming, 'Shoplifter!'

I screamed, too, and people gathered round to help me. I was, after all, just a kid. In all the madness the woman's wig flew off, but she didn't care. She held me down until three security guards arrived. They hauled me to a back room, where I had to sit until the police arrived.

I was petrified of my mother's reaction, since she had given me the money specifically for the groceries, so I threw a tantrum, trying to get out of the room. I kicked and screamed but Mum, Dad and the police came anyway.

The police were kinder than my parents were. They let me off with a caution, since I was so young and it was my first offence. My parents gave me a good thrashing when we got home. Where was that protecting presence now? It had warned me about the baby birds, but I suppose I couldn't expect it to help me out of the mischief I got into myself.

4

In the early 1960s, the government had undertaken a development programme in the Skelmersdale neighbourhood where I lived in an attempt to house the overspill of the population from Liverpool. On paper, it must have seemed like a good idea, but they uprooted people, dumped them in the council estate and then failed to develop the infrastructure. There was nothing to amuse this transplanted population, especially the young people. To make matters worse, several of the area's largest industrial employers moved out of the area in the late 1970s, tipping Skelmersdale into a tailspin of poverty, drug abuse, weapons, violence and gangs.

I was experiencing this all too closely – right outside my own front door. I knew about the gangs from my older brother, Tommy. He was a member of the Digmoor Nutter Troop (DNT), the first and largest of the three gangs in Skelmersdale. Gang territories were divided according to where you lived. Entire families were stuck with the gang from their area; they could not switch allegiance at will. That meant I was in the DNT gang.

The other gangs were a rough one called the Tanhouse Riot Squad (TRS), and the New Church Farm Boys (NCFB) which was made up of older men a generation ahead of Tommy. Add those to the gangs in the surrounding towns such as Wigan and Kirby, and we lived in constant fear, in the midst of gang warfare wherever we went.

The gangs patrolled and protected their territories and wouldn't hesitate to attack anyone who ventured on to their turf. Knives and baseball bats were the weapons of choice. Fortunately, guns were not yet widely available.

Since I'd grown up in Digmoor territory and was Tommy's younger brother, the big boys looked out for me and my mates. I could strut around town with my head held high as long as I had my friends or older lads around me. When I was alone, though, I was terrified.

When I was eleven I went to St Richard's Secondary School, which was about a mile from my house. I hated junior school, and knew this new school would be even harder. I had heard all the horror stories about secondary school and braced myself for the first day.

I didn't leave my hell-raising behaviour behind in junior school. Most of my DNT gang members and the rival gangs from other parts of Skelmersdale merged at this new school into one wild and warring world.

The very first day, we all scrapped for position and power. No one dared let down their guard because that would show vulnerability, and wimps were brutally battered. Tough guys like me were not in class to learn. I was constantly on edge, watching my back and ready to put up my fists for the next scuffle.

That day, my worst fears were realized. I was minding my own business when a tough-looking lad shouted at me, 'Who are you?'

Trying to rise above the situation, I casually said, 'Joe.'

The lad and his mates doubled over in laughter. 'Piss off then!' he said.

I felt my blood begin to bubble and yelled, 'Fuck off!' Then I saw the guy jump forward and try to punch me. Saved by the school bell, I bolted to my classroom but, throughout the day, my thoughts kept returning to what had happened. What if these lads tried to beat me up after school? I devised escape plans in my mind but dreaded the thought of facing this danger every day.

At lunch, I was heading to a table with my sandwich when I heard one of the lads who had threatened me shout, 'Joooeeey, you're dead after school.'

I managed to keep my cool, even though I was terrified inside. The boy had a reputation for violence, and I didn't want to be his first victim at secondary school.

The rest of the day was terrible; I spent it thinking about the beating I was facing. I didn't dare tell the teacher, or I'd be labelled a grass. The gang rule was: you don't tell on anybody.

My heart rate skyrocketed when the final bell rang and the teacher announced it was home time. My entire body felt drained of blood as I filtered between my friends walking out of school. I hoped I was hidden among them and tried to act cocky and brave. I made it to the subway, which was halfway home, and was almost feeling that I had made it when I heard a menacing voice.

'There he is, Danny! Let's get Bolster!'

I whipped around and saw fifteen to twenty kids raging towards me. Within seconds, I was surrounded. Their bodies formed a ring around Danny and me, all of them taking a front-row seat for my beating.

All of a sudden, I felt a mighty blow to my head and collapsed on the street. It was followed by kicks to my face and head. I was half conscious and unable to focus on a way to fight back or protect myself.

In my numbed state, I faintly heard Danny's voice: 'C'mon, Bolster. Stand up and fight.' The haunting laughs from the other boys sounded muffled in my brain.

Suddenly, my mind went blank and an incredible calmness infused my entire body. I heard a familiar male voice: 'Get up, son. Fight back. Get up now.'

Instantly, I had the energy of an ox and I leapt up from the ground with a force so powerful, I was amazed by it. I have no idea where this Herculean strength came from, but I clenched my fists, drew back and punched Danny on the chin like a boxer. My anger took over and, with my confidence intact, I went on hitting him until he begged me to stop.

I shook myself back into reality and slowly drew away. We were both panting like dogs.

The lads backed away in alarm, then took off running.

Alone now and gasping, I bent over, my hands on my knees, trying to catch my breath. Where in the hell did I get that surge of energy to retaliate?

I slowly straightened my aching body and felt a hand leaning hard on my shoulder. I whirled around, praying this wasn't round two. I was alone. Then a loud voice boomed off the walls of the subway.

'Well done, son. You stood your ground.'

Tears filled my eyes. It was Great-uncle Tom. I remembered hearing his voice when I was blacked out on the pavement. I was overcome with emotion and gratitude that he was with me, offering guidance and protection, since there was nobody else who understood my situation. Now, I had utter trust in his assistance and hoped he would stay with me for ever.

The next day at school, the bullies ignored me.

Soon after I started at St Richard's Secondary School, my parents wanted a change, so they asked the council to move us to Runcorn, where some of Dad's relatives lived. It was a good twenty-five miles from Skelmersdale, and we were all hoping for a better life, away from the constant violence of the Skelmersdale streets.

I enrolled at Halton Secondary School, which I quickly came to hate. Even though St Richard's was little more than a war zone, with territory fought over by the various gangs, this new school had a nasty feel to it that I couldn't put my finger on. I felt spirits in the corridors and had a horrible vision of a person drowning in the canal near the school. And the grounds were really creepy.

I did meet a new friend called Scottie. We both got jobs delivering milk, eggs and bread with the milkman in the nearby housing estates. I had a special friendship with Scottie, and we earned up to £3 a week in tips.

It turned out that Runcorn did not impress the Bolster family. Mum and Dad hated the area, and after just four months of living there, they decided to buy their own home, back in Skelmersdale. Most families found houses through the council, and it was a bold move to forgo the government subsidy and pay for a home on your own. Most people just did not have that kind of money. Mum and Dad found a house in an area called Carfield, just a minute away from the old house with the fabulous garden, and this became the new family home.

There was one problem though. St Richard's was full and couldn't take any more students so, at the age of twelve, I was sent to West Bank Secondary School.

Back in Skelmersdale, I had a mate named Quinny who came from a broken home and had grown up in care. He had been in trouble with the police for burglaries and other sorts of roguery, so now he lived in the local children's home.

'I'm gonna be a millionaire by the time I'm thirty,' he bragged. I was impressed with his swagger, and with the various gems of wisdom he offered me and the other lads.

Quinny's girlfriend, Diane, had a friend called Susan. Susan's mother was into Ouija boards and spent hours communicating with spirits, who supposedly spelled out messages on the board. One day, Quinny went to Susan's house to pick up Diane.

'Come upstairs and meet my mum,' Susan said, knowing full well she was on the Ouija board.

After great hesitation, Quinny climbed the stairs behind Diane and, when they entered one of the bedrooms, he saw a woman sitting there holding a clear drinking glass over a lettered board. He had heard about Ouija boards before and could see the glass moving at a fair pace. As Quinny approached the woman, the glass went haywire, zooming around the board and spelling out dire warnings about him.

Susan's mother let out a piercing scream which made them all jump. 'The spirits say you're a robber ... a ... a ... thief and ... b-u-r-glar,' she read, as the glass spelled out the last word. 'Get out of my house!'

'Mum, Quinny's nice,' Susan said, trying to calm her down. 'Leave him alone!'

Quinny turned and fled down the stairs with Diane and Susan in hot pursuit. Quinny was wearing his beloved blue puffa jacket with the big pockets, and Susan told him to run home as fast as he could, the whole mile to the children's home.

'If anything strange happens, rip off your coat and throw it down,' Susan warned. 'Any bad entity that may have attached to you will be flung off with the coat.'

Quinny was scared out of his mind but, trying to maintain his tough reputation, he kissed Diane goodbye, trying to look cool and unfazed by the whole thing. But, outside, in the darkness, his blood rose in panic, and he legged it as fast as he could, hoping to shake off any ghosts that had stuck with him. His mind ran amok, picturing a demon ready to pounce as he panted and pounded his way down the street.

He jammed his hands into his jacket pockets and freaked out when his right hand touched something gooey and sticky. His terrified mind pictured some kind of ectoplasm oozing through his fingers, so he yanked his hand out of his pocket and wiggled out of the jacket, throwing it aside as he raced towards the home.

The jacket was gone, but there was still something on his hand, so he thought that meant he was now possessed. His heart ready to burst, he collapsed against a lamp post, fighting for breath. He cried in fright at the sight of his fingers, stuck together with a thick, white slime.

Then he smelled a strong, familiar sweetness. He sniffed his fingers – and that's when he remembered the Cadbury's Creme Egg he had bought before he picked up Diane. He'd lost his famous puffa jacket, and the story became legendary among my mates.

Soon afterwards, however, I had my own scary encounter with a Ouija board.

That school year my gang hung out with some girls from Digmoor. I got on well with girls and enjoyed their company. One afternoon, a group of them invited me to join them for a whirl on a Ouija board.

I made fun of the idea because I didn't believe in the things, especially after what had happened to Quinny. But, wanting to be with the girls, I followed them to an empty house to give it a try. The abandoned house was scary enough and, oddly, there was already a table sitting in the middle of the living room. We set the board on the table and all gathered round. I was with seven girls and I figured there had to be safety in numbers. We placed our fingers lightly on the glass and it immediately whizzed across the board. It was downright spooky.

I swear it spelled out D-E-A-T-H; then it began to spell our names. It jerked around the board at a dizzying speed.

'Joe, stop moving it!' one girl said.

'I swear I'm not,' I said, trying to keep my fingers on the speeding glass.

'Yes you are!' the other girls protested.

I could not explain what was happening but I knew I was not consciously moving that glass. Suddenly, it flew out of our hands and smashed against the ceiling, raining spiky shards all over us.

We freaked out. The only way out of the boarded-up house was to squeeze under a board and slide out. Seven screaming girls and I broke the sound barrier in our panic to escape. We ran home, just like Quinny had that time. I wondered later if I did have something to do with that moving glass – not deliberately, but maybe it was one of those ghosts that hung around me.

Now that I have embraced my psychic gifts, I understand Ouija boards. They are indeed a means of communication between earth and the spirit world and have been used for centuries. If you use them with a positive attitude, you can attract upbeat spirits. The danger comes with people who suffer low self-esteem and contact negative energies or lower life spirits.

My advice is to use Ouija boards with a loving and positive outlook; then you should enjoy loving and positive results.

The following year, Margaret Thatcher was elected prime minister. The government started selling off council houses to tenants, and tenants made up the majority of Skelmersdale residents.

I became a mini-mogul, determined to create my own little financial empire and cash in on the change. Money was still my sole goal. I gathered my mates together to scour empty houses. When we learned someone was moving in, we stripped whatever we could, ripping windows from their frames, cutting out copper piping, pinching plumbing fixtures – you name it. I'd then offer to sell these items back to the home buyer at a big discount, compared to regular stores. They thought they were getting a good deal.

I ran the operation and told my mates what to do. The average takings netted £125 and, with four to five house strippings a week, I was raking in a fortune. It was easy money. Not only did I have excellent workers, I had plenty of customers. The business got so busy and was so lucrative that I had trouble keeping up with it.

It came to a shocking end when a man moving into his new house offered me £75 for an electric meter. That was a ton of money back in those days. I sneaked into an empty house with some large wire-cutters, thinking it would be brilliant to earn that much money for virtually no effort. Unfortunately, I had absolutely no understanding of electricity. I just wanted the box, so I cut into the thick wires.

I felt a jolt and my body flew across the room, landing in a heap. I opened my eyes, seeing stars – in fact, tiny lights flickering all around me – and my entire body ached. Smoke fumed from my hair. I'm sure I looked like a madman, and I was still holding the cutters in my hand. I now know I was lucky to survive, although I do even now occasionally wonder whether this primitive electro-shock therapy amplified my psychic ability in some way.

When I was thirteen, the police caught me shoplifting some clothes, and this time I was ordered to do community service at Hindley Mornington Secondary School. It's hard to believe, but I was actually proud to face this sentence and thought it would prove I was hard and tough. But the moment I stepped into the place, I had the shock of my life. This was no typical school; it was an ex-army boot camp.

I was sentenced to attend the boot camp every Saturday for eight weeks and, while I was there, I and the other attendees were made to perform gruelling physical exercises. I thought I was fit, but I could barely stomach the countless crunches, push-ups and, worst of all, the running. After one lengthy jog, I puked in the grass. I felt sorry for one overweight kid who was sweating like a pig. After only a day of this torture, I decided I didn't have the stamina for this punishment.

That night, Great-uncle Tom visited me in a dream. 'Fake an injury,' he told me. It was a brilliant idea, and I was disappointed I hadn't thought of it myself.

The next week, I purposely tripped during a run and faked a broken arm. They hauled me to hospital, where I held my arm dead still and convinced them I needed a cast. The doctor wrote a note that excused me from the exercises.

I still had to complete my stint at boot camp but, instead of exercising and working outside in the cold, I was assigned to the office, where I answered the phones. Every so often I would look out of the window and feel sorry for the fat kid, still out there having to do the exercises.

I was thrilled when classes finally ended that year and I was off school for the next six weeks. Summer was my favourite time of year, with the warm weather and freedom from studies. One day at the beginning of our holiday, the doorbell rang.

'Joe, your mate Colin is here,' Mum shouted up the stairs.

I was ready for an adventure, and I knew Colin would help me find it that day. We clunked down the steps and out of the house.

'Don't be late for tea,' Mum called after us as we headed down the street.

'What shall we do today?' I asked Colin, and he suggested we go to the monks' – our name for the local monastery – even though it was a good three-mile walk away. I loved the monastery because there was a real sense of history about it, and Colin and I enjoyed digging for valuable old bottles dating back hundreds of years. We sold the bottles to local antique dealers for a few pennies.

But that day, the moment we started digging, the monastery's security guard caught us and chased us off the property. 'If I catch you here again, I'll call the police,' he scolded.

We were so cheeky, we laughed in his face, then

hot-tailed it out of there, disappointed that he had spoiled our fun.

Still in search of excitement, we walked to the lake to watch the local fishermen. I had always had a fascination with fishing, and Abbey Lakes in Up Holland attracted all the local anglers. I started to feel hungry and, since we had no money, we resorted to a street tactic. We approached one of the fishermen who had a fresh loaf of bread.

'Please, sir,' Colin said. 'Can we have some of your bread to feed the ducks?'

'Sure,' the angler said, and cut off four slices.

We hurried out of sight and ate the bread ourselves. We were about to head home when Colin noticed what looked like a derelict house across the road from the pond on Orrell Road. The dirty red-brick house stood alone, the roof sagging and parts of it already collapsed. Shutters barricaded the windows and ivy crawled over the structure. The garden was so overgrown that the footpath was covered over. The whole place looked as if it had been long forgotten, unvisited by anyone for at least twenty years, and its being so close to the graveyard added to its creepy atmosphere.

I stood outside the property and had a sudden feeling of déjà vu, as if I had been to the house before, even though that was impossible. Somehow, it looked familiar. It was approaching dusk, and I knew my mother would be looking for me soon to join the family for tea, but the house drew me in.

Colin and I made our way along the side of the house,

where we discovered an old wooden garage. We peeped through the door and found what looked like a 1950s Ford, covered in dust and cobwebs. We jumped over a decaying brick wall to take a closer look. I licked my finger and wiped it over the wheel arch; underneath, the black paint glowed. The huge round chrome headlights and the massive dials on the dashboard set my heart pumping. I would have killed to own and drive that car.

The sun was setting fast, but we made our way to the front door, where we found two cold glass bottles of milk.

'That's odd,' I said to Colin. 'Who would deliver fresh milk to an abandoned house?' We peeled off one of the foil tops and sniffed the milk. It smelled fine, so we took a sip. It was delicious, so we took turns gulping it down, which gave us some more energy, after the bread.

'Let's go in,' I suggested.

'No way! That house is haunted.'

I shoved Colin from behind and led him round to the back, where I pushed open the creaky door. We stepped into what must have been the kitchen. Wind whistled through the open door and blew dust across the floor. The dingy kitchen reeked of damp, rotting wood. It was so pungent, it took our breath away.

'God, I can't stand the smell in here,' Colin complained, clamping his nose.

'Shut up,' I said, and went on exploring the room. The kitchen stove still stood on the cold stone floor, black with dirt. A cobweb draped itself across my face, and I coughed when my scream sucked it into my mouth. It freaked me out, but I was trying to keep my cool in front of Colin because he was older than me. My adrenaline surged. I was frightened, but my excitement pushed me to move onwards.

The moment we entered the living room, fright hit me in the stomach. A commanding voice in my mind shouted at me: 'Don't go any further! Leave now!' Suddenly, I felt sick.

Colin stumbled over some rotting newspapers that were piled up on the damp carpet and made his way to the stairs. 'I'm going up,' he said.

'No!' I yelled. The voice screamed at me again to get out of the house. 'Colin, let's go!'

Instantly, I knew we were not alone there. There was someone upstairs, and whoever it was was very angry with us. The voice was so forceful it was overwhelming, and a series of flashing visions made me dizzy. I could feel and smell death.

Colin crept up the stairs. I knew I had to follow, but a mist appeared, clouding him out of my sight. The fog formed into a man and a woman, who dived towards me with stabbing eyes.

'Leave now! Get out of this house!' they shrieked.

I was scared out of my mind and now I could hear Colin screaming upstairs – 'Joe, help me!' – but I just couldn't climb those stairs. I bolted out of the house, leaving Colin behind. I ran all the way home and was too distraught to eat any of my tea.

I didn't tell anyone what had happened, and I didn't see Colin for days. I was convinced he was dead. He had been murdered and I had left him to die. When I walked past his house, the curtains were drawn shut. I was over-come with a sense of guilt and horror.

Three days later, I was walking down the road, still overwrought with anxiety, when Colin rounded a corner. He was covered from head to toe in bruises. I can't describe how relieved I was to see my mate alive, even though he called me a bastard for leaving him. He told me that a hermit lived upstairs in the house and that, when he had caught Colin, he had kicked him all over his body with his heavy boots. Colin had struggled and managed to get away.

Later, we learned that the hermit's name was Tommy Williams. The story went that Tommy had seen his parents killed years before and had gone crazy. He and his sister, Ilynn, just carried on living in the house, in total isolation and in deplorable conditions, for years. The house was infested with rats and polluted with human faeces. Eventually, social services made them leave the house and they both died in care in 2002.

The Orrell Road hermits' house was a legend in the area, and there were numerous scary stories of what went on within those eerie walls. The decrepit house was finally torn down in February 2007. Someone said that the floorboards had been so rotten that the family piano had plunged into the cellar.

I hadn't known anything about the history of the house when Colin and I stumbled upon it. When I found out about it later, I wondered if it had been the parents in the mist warning me to flee.

5

When classes started up again late that summer, second-ary school continued with fights and the constant struggle to earn and retain respect among the various tough boys and gangs. It wasn't easy, especially combined with my additional burden of spirit visitors and visions.

When I was fourteen, I was on the train from Black-pool to Wigan when I noticed a lad about the same age as me. I knew him; it was Alan Jones from Skelmersdale. His uncle was a notorious gangster, and Alan was mixed up with guns, drugs and gangs. That was the environment within which many young boys in my area grew up, and I hung out with them. I understood the way Alan thought, and that he didn't know anything different.

He sat down in the seat beside me. 'How are you?' he asked. 'What are you doing in this area?'

I replied that my dad had sent me to Fleetwood to buy marine fish for his aquarium.

Alan was on his way home from the young offenders' institution where he was doing time for rowdy behaviour and for having had several run-ins with the police. We chatted easily for the next two hours. He was a real hard case, and I knew he was the type to turn on anyone. I was well aware of the gang personality, and Alan was one of the toughest of them.

As we talked, a strange thing began to happen. My mind altered in some way, and I fell virtually comatose. I could see Alan's lips moving in conversation, but I no longer heard him. I felt strange, dazed, a state I had not experienced before, and it was disconcerting.

It felt as if I had been sitting in this condition for a long while when, suddenly, the blackness in my mind expanded into an image. It was as if I were watching a mini-movie in my head. The main character was Alan, and he was standing in the middle of the screen, guns spinning and flying around his head.

The scene changed. Alan, now older, was standing in the midst of what looked like a massacre. The story became clear, and I saw that Alan had shot and killed a man. The pace of the movie quickened and, in a matter of moments, I saw Alan's repulsive future – money, gangsters, women, drugs and crime – flashing before me. I shook my head, trying to stop the barrage of images, but they played out to the end.

Finally they faded and I returned to the present, back to the sounds of the train. It took me a moment to shake the fog from my head and realize that Alan was sitting inches away from me, with no idea that I had just witnessed his future. I'd had glimpses before of things that had not yet happened, such as the warning not to go up the stairs in the hermit's house, but this was my first full-blown premonition. I was stunned and frightened. Should I tell Alan that he was at some point going to kill someone?

My heart was hammering in my chest as I puzzled

things over. The movie had no button to push to pause or stop it from playing. I'd had no choice but to sit and watch it spool out. I had complete confidence that what had happened in the movie was true and that I had witnessed Alan's destiny. And what made it even more terrifying was that I had no idea where or when it would happen. I didn't have the nerve to say anything to him and could barely focus as he carried on talking about his current life, aged thirteen.

Of course, Alan did continue in his gangster ways, but years passed before the premonition played itself out in reality. I was shocked when I read a headline in the newspaper in August 2002: DRUG BARON JAILED FOR MURDER. Alan's picture blazed from the front page.

According to the article, Alan was one of Lancashire's most dangerous drug barons and controlled a multi-million-pound crime empire. He had shot a rival gangster, Ricky Bates, in the head in front of numerous witnesses in broad daylight.

'He showed no remorse, only lofty arrogance,' the judge had said. 'He treated the law with contempt.'

Alan was also convicted of attempted murder and various drug offences and now faces decades in prison.

The paper quoted the detective chief inspector as saying that there was no doubt that Alan Jones was a very dangerous and extremely violent individual, and that the people of Lancashire would be much safer without him at liberty.

At the time of his arrest, he was building a half-million-pound luxury mansion in Skelmersdale. The article gave me a real shock – my premonition had come true.

Another time when I was fourteen, I remember sitting in the house watching television. My nine-year-old brother Denny was laid out on the couch, his curly mop of hair moving as he breathed. He wasn't well and the doctor came to give him a check-up. I had a sense that he had something more than the virus the doctor had diagnosed, and a sudden vision showed me our Denny in hospital.

That night I was in the top bunk, as usual, with Denny and Johnny in the bed below me. Mum was up to check on Denny several times during the night. On her fourth visit, she noticed that Denny's skin was covered in bruises. She called the doctor out again, and Denny was rushed to hospital at about six in the morning.

It turned out that my younger brother had meningitis, pneumonia and septicaemia, all potentially fatal conditions. The doctors told Mum that if she had waited any longer to get Denny to hospital, he would have died. At this point, he had a fifty–fifty chance of surviving.

I remember it was Dad's birthday around that time, and the only present he wanted was for Denny to get better. He prayed and prayed.

I was frightened, but I felt a certain peace about the outcome, and I was learning to trust my instincts. Sure enough, after ten days, Denny's condition started to improve.

*

Now that I was a teen, I had a keener view and understanding of Skelmersdale. Alongside the poverty, there was a general atmosphere of fear. Active gang members were rough and tough on the outside but scared to death on the inside. To cope, drugs such as magic mushrooms, cannabis, acid, ketamine, cocaine and alcohol were in high demand and were used regularly both to fuel aggression and to calm nerves.

The girls were involved with the gangs, too, including my own sisters. One evening, I was out with my mates in an area called Tanhouse, about a half mile from where I lived. We were looking for girls to chat up when we came across a gang of teenagers hanging outside a block of flats. As we approached, I saw my sisters, Diane and Tracey.

'Does Mum know you're with these gangs?' I asked.

'Yes! Yes!' they shouted, trying to act cool in front of the older lads who were drinking cider with who knows what mixed with it. Both Diane and Tracey took a sip, and I noticed they were flirting.

'You better not be dating any of these lads,' I warned Tracey.

'Oh, shut up, Joe!' Tracey was three years older than me, and Diane had just turned sixteen. My mates laughed at me for warning my big sisters.

I sensed that this gang of lads was tamer than my own gang, so I asked one of the guys his name. He told me it was Graham.

'Where are you from?' His accent was different to ours.

'Great Yarmouth. I'm visiting my dad, who lives in this block of flats.' He took a long swig of the cider.

Suddenly, I felt a cold chill. It seemed Tracey and Diane had been hanging out with these gang members for a while now, and I had a creepy feeling about Graham's dad's flat. I managed to talk my sisters into leaving and, as we walked home, they admitted that they had lied to Mum, telling her they were off to a disco that evening.

'How was the disco?' Mum asked as we entered the house.

Tracey and Diane squirmed with nerves, wondering if I would grass on them – Mum would have gone mad if she had known they were hanging out with boys in gangs – but I covered for them.

That night, I fell into a deep sleep in my top bunk. In a dream, I drifted out of my bed and found myself hovering over the bunk looking down at myself. I was shocked and amazed to be out of my body; I had never done this in my sleep before. I moved around the room, left my bedroom and floated down the stairs. I was soon drifting down the streets of Skelmersdale, and I glided to the block of flats where I had seen my sisters earlier that evening.

What happened next frightened me to the core. I transported myself inside Graham's dad's flat and was blinded by flashing cameras in the darkened room. The whole atmosphere alarmed me. I was floating around what I realized was a bedroom and was shocked to see a young girl about my age on the bed, dressed only in her underwear. An older man with a beard was taking provocative pictures of her, ordering the girl to move around and contort her body as he did so.

The image dissolved quickly, and my body was sucked out of the room, out of the flat, down the street and back into my top bunk.

'Wake up, Joe.' My mother was shaking me. 'You over-slept.'

That evening, I returned to the block of flats in Tanhouse and found my sisters hanging out with the same gang of guys. They winced when they saw me, but invited me up to one of the flats. The steps up to it reeked of urine, and I had an odd feeling when we entered Graham's dad's apartment. I asked to use the bathroom, but instead had a look around. I couldn't believe it when I went into the bedroom and found several cameras aimed at the bed. The walls were plastered with lewd shots of young girls. It was the exact same room I had seen in my astral-travel visit!

I hurried out of the room and walked into the living room just as an older man came through the front door. I froze in shock. He was the man with the beard I had seen in the dream. I intuitively knew my sisters were in danger and hurried them out of the house. Back home, I told Dad what I had seen in the flat. He forbade my sisters ever to go there again.

Several months later, a picture of the bearded man was plastered all over the front page of the newspaper. He had been arrested for enticing young girls to his home and taking the vulgar photos.

When I turned fifteen, I started to experience a strange new phenomenon. One of my best mates at the time was

Brian Edwards, who was two years older than me. We used to hang out at a pub called the Almond Tree.

One day, as I was sitting across from Brian at one of the tables in the pub, he was suddenly surrounded by an odd haze. I stared at him in awe as the grey mist expanded around him. I began to see visions flashing in front of Brian, showing me his future. I saw him with a girlfriend and two children. Then I had an image of him falling out with his girlfriend, and her leaving him. Then, to my amazement, I witnessed him killing himself.

I tried to shake off this frightening premonition. It was the first time I had seen a grey vapour around someone. I couldn't imagine Brian committing suicide because he was a happy, carefree person. I hated having seen into his future, with its gruesome conclusion. I didn't have the nerve to tell anyone, but the image haunted me for years.

The grey mist visited again one time when I was sitting in the headmaster's office at West Bank Secondary. I never concentrated in school and was often sent to the headmaster to be disciplined, but Mr Litham was a genuinely decent guy. He was strict but, that day, he told me I had great potential, if I would only apply myself to my studies.

Surprisingly for me back then, I was actually listening to what he had to say, but then I fell into a trance-like state. The grey haze started to rise and eventually cloaked him. This aura seemed to be communicating with me. I saw Mr Litham grab his chest as if in crushing pain, and then I saw him lying on the ground. These visions were outside my mind, as if I were watching them on television.

The whole thing lasted less than a minute, and I was left staring at him. He was only in his mid to late forties.

A week later, I had a fight with a guy in my woodwork class. I ended up with an impressive black eye and was taken to hospital. While lying in bed there, I had a vision of my woodwork teacher surrounded by the grey haze. The aura showed me a vision of him also holding his chest, then a flash of a funeral.

Imagine the shock I had a few weeks later when I heard that both the headmaster and my woodwork teacher were dead of heart attacks! I was staggered at the accuracy of my premonitions and the grey mist. After that, if I saw the grey fog around somebody, I knew it meant they were in ill health, near death or had been to a funeral.

About five years later, I received more dramatic news. My old friend Brian Edwards had broken up with his girlfriend and was so distraught he had hanged himself, leaving behind two children.

It wasn't just grey mists I saw, though. I saw colourful ones around certain people. I would be in a crowd or in the playground when somebody would light up as if a bulb had been turned on inside them. I didn't know at the time that I was seeing auras, the electromagnetic field that is around every person and every thing. I was tapping into this energy in a big way.

Every time an aura appeared, the colour was beyond this world. The reds, pinks and greens glowed with an intensity and shine much more powerful than the colours we see on earth. The auras poured information into me but, at that point, I didn't know what to do with it.

That school year, I had my eye on a lovely girl called Jemima. Her head was surrounded with a beautiful white halo. The light told me that Jemima really fancied me. I jumped on that intuition, and we began to hang out together. I used to visit her house and grew fond of her mum, too – she was so friendly. When I began to see a man standing behind Jemima's mother, it scared me. He was much older than she was, and I sensed he was a grandfather. I never told Jemima or her mother about this spirit visitor. In an odd coincidence, Jemima left me after a year and began dating Alan Jones, the gangster about whom I had had a premonition earlier!

As I have said, throughout my entire childhood I was totally alone with my visions, voices and premonitions. I never came across anyone who had the same experiences I did. One day, when I was fifteen, I remember walking with my sister Diane in the nearby town of Pimbo. We were picking blackberries, which grew wild along the hedgerow at the edge of a field. I was having a great time.

Diane and I glanced over the hedge and saw a tiny old thatched cottage in the field. A nun in a black habit was standing at the window and waving at us. We smiled and waved back. We carried on, enjoying picking the berries and, when we had finished, Diane and I looked over at the house to see if the nun was still watching us. Both the house and the nun were gone. They had totally vanished!

My sister let out a terrified shriek that almost burst my eardrums. 'Joe, you *did* see that little house and the nun, didn't you?' she begged.

Indeed I had seen them both, but I now realized that the cottage and the nun had been one of my visions, and I was amazed that my sister had seen them too. Much later, I learned that visions like this are actually projections from the past. The nun had probably lived on that land centuries ago, and we had tuned into her imprint.

That day, Diane broke down and told me that she had started having visions when she was about ten and was petrified by them. Like me, she saw spirits and visions in school and at home and experienced upsetting pre-monitions.

I started to chuckle, and she punched me in the arm. I was so elated that I was no longer alone with this bizarre phenomenon, now so common for me. 'Diane, you can tell the spirits to go away,' I soothed. 'You can actually switch them off.' I knew this wasn't always true.

She was relieved to hear that I understood. Diane was just a year older than me, and we had always been close.

Diane is now a highly gifted psychic. To this day, she is afraid of her abilities and has nightmares about dolls. She encourages me in my work as a medium/psychic, but has not embraced her own gift.

I understood her terror, because I continued to fear many aspects of my own psychic make-up. That same year, I remember looking in the mirror and falling into a trance-like state. I saw my own auric field. The more I stared, the more my heart sank. The reflection clearly showed that I was lost, with no direction or pathway in my life. I was obviously on the wrong road. Then, sud-denly, I saw an elderly woman standing behind me. She was tiny and looked ancient. I ran from the room in fright and wouldn't look in a mirror again for years. I was always afraid I would see her again.

I felt really low after that. I truly was in a rut, and I was still getting into trouble with the police. I usually ended up on probation or community service, where my punishment was to cut grass.

When I was coming to the end of secondary school, a spirit woman visited me in dreams eight to ten times over a period of five months. She called herself Nan, but she wasn't my grandmother.

'I wanted to meet you, Joe,' she said. 'My name is Mary.'

She was a very kindly spirit. She was old, but nice-looking, with light brown hair, lovely cheekbones and blue eyes. She said she was looking out for me. 'Your dad is coming to see you soon,' she said. I was puzzled. I lived with my dad, so why would he be coming for a visit soon?

I finally confided in Diane about Mary, and she began to cry. 'Joe, Mary is your real grandmother.' Talk about a shock! I was so young when Mum had left Jackie Power that I didn't remember him.

A few weeks later, Diane and Tracey were in a pub when a young woman walked up to them and handed them a note. It turned out that my real father had had more kids after us and now wanted to see us again. Although hesitant, my sisters and Tommy went to meet him in a pub.

When he saw them, my father said he had tried to get

in touch with us lots of times. 'Where is Joe?' he asked, apparently. 'I want to see Joe.'

Tommy told me this and gave me the option of going to meet my father, but I never contacted him. Mary returned in a dream and told me that she understood why I didn't want to see him but that she still wanted to be my nan and to watch over me.

When I finally finished secondary school at the age of sixteen, I signed up for the Youth Training Scheme (YTS), which was a government initiative designed to steer youth out of unemployment and into the workplace. They offered £25 a week, a tiny amount. I signed up for the cookery course, but my real interest was gardening, so I soon switched to that.

The classes were held in an old building, and I regularly saw spirits there. One day, while sitting at lunch with some girls, I saw a flash of mist and a quick build-up of a body forming. It swiftly became the full body of a man sitting in the canteen. This is how most of the spirits manifested themselves. I knew they were spirits because I saw them forming but, once they were in their full body, they looked like any other human.

I now know it takes tremendous energy for spirits to show themselves on earth, and that's why the images do not last long. This spirit melted away rapidly, like the others.

Another time, I was eating tea in my mum's kitchen when I had a sudden vision of people kicking me and me lying in some water.

The scene played itself out in reality a few days later when five or six lads from my gardening class decided to bully me. They came at me with their boots and kicked me, just like in my premonition. Then they lifted me bodily and hauled me to a stream that was in the grounds where the gardening class took place and dumped me in it.

I was worried I would die. Why else would I have been forewarned of this attack? Of course, I lived and, a few days later, I managed to get my own back on one of them, cornering him and kicking him in turn.

After that encounter, I left the YTS scheme. I ran away from home without telling Mum or Dad and made my way down to Bournemouth to join Tracey and Tommy. They now shared a flat there, and picked up whatever jobs they could find – at fast-food restaurants and hotels. They had very little money and lived in a seedy little flat in a road called Crabton Close. Lots of their mates lived nearby and, although my brother and sister did not partake, there were drugs everywhere.

When I arrived, I met up with an old friend named Steven Allen. One summer night, we sneaked out. We walked along in the dark for about half a mile and came across a row of flats. We looked up and, in one of the large picture windows, I clearly saw a man hanging by his neck from the chandelier. Steven screamed and collapsed in hysterics. I, on the other hand, was for some reason mesmerized by the man's expensive brown suit and crisp white shirt. They actually glowed on his body.

We took off down the street, squealing like schoolgirls.

Steven stopped to catch his breath. 'We … we … have to call the police,' he gasped.

I laughed at this tough guy, who now looked like a frightened puppy. 'We saw what we saw … he's fuckin' hanging there!'

Steven pleaded. 'We have to go back.'

We returned to the flat, and I was not at all surprised when we gazed into the window and the hanging man was gone. Steven, however, almost fainted. It had just been a vision. The hanging man had intuited to me that he was in his seventies and had recently lost his wife. He was too lonely to live without her, so he killed himself.

Back at Tom and Tracey's flat, Steven shared the story with some friends who had gathered there. Most of them were smoking pot, and they laughed and sputtered at Steven's tale. I wouldn't have said anything about it because I was used to seeing spirits. I was just glad to know that Steven had seen the vision too.

6

Shortly after I had arrived in Bournemouth, I was in my sister and brother's flat, lying on the bed. I had no money and knew I needed to find a job. Across my mind flashed a vision of myself – locked behind bars.

A few weeks later, I met a bloke called Jacko, a six-foot-five giant who was well known to the police because of the numerous burglaries he had committed. We were both flat broke, and one evening he asked if I wanted to help him on a job.

'I'll do the pinchin',' he said. 'You only have to be the lookout and watch for the police.'

As the sun began to set, Jacko and I approached one of the classy hotels in the town. He scuttled up the steps but was immediately chased away by security guards. We walked on to another hotel and spotted a shed on the property. Jacko was so tall and gangly, he reached over the fence easily and opened the gate.

'Watch the road,' he said. 'I'm going to break into the shed.' Jacko quickly snapped the padlock with a screwdriver and, inside the shed, he found several freezers full of food. He shouted me over and began passing me bags of sausages and scampi. The load was heavy and, of course, freezing. Soon I had ice-cold bags stacked up to my chin.

As we hauled our booty off the grounds, both weighed down by our loads, I grew anxious in case we were caught. My arms were freezing and starting to ache. Close by, we spotted a row of bedsits, one of which we knew was occupied by an eccentric woman who dressed like Boy George. I knew she fancied me, so we knocked on her door and, when she answered, we lugged in our loot.

Anyone from my economic background would have been delighted to see so much food. We shared some of it with the woman and were feeling very proud of ourselves – until the next day, when the police came round looking for a tall, skinny guy and a short, scrawny lad.

They hauled us off to Bournemouth police station. We were denied bail because of Jacko's form, and it was our bad luck that the police were having a crackdown on what had become a rash of break-ins in the town.

I lied and pleaded not guilty but was slapped into HM Prison, Portland, Dorset, which was also used as a remand centre, to await trial. I spent four months there until our trial began, in Bournemouth's crown court.

The prosecution had no evidence against us, but it did have a star witness. Jacko and I wondered if the hotel's security had seen us, but imagine our surprise when the Boy George lookalike took the stand! What a grass – and after we had shared our food with her, too.

She wasn't very bright, and smiled and giggled on the stand.

'Do you recognize either of these lads?' the prosecutor asked. She pointed to Jacko.

'I know him.'

I stared at her. She obviously wasn't all there

'Do you know this man?' The prosecutor pointed at me.

She smiled coyly. 'No, I don't.' Thank goodness, she was standing up for me.

It didn't work, though. Jacko and I were both convicted, and the judge sentenced me to eighteen months in Portland Young Offenders' Institution, since I was still only seventeen. The prison was on an island, so there wasn't much chance of escape, and anyone who did try was captured by the Royal Air Force.

The prison was built in 1848, and conditions were squalid. Rats scampered about in the food-service area, the showers were rarely cleaned properly and were caked with years of accumulated filth, and the whole place stank of urine. Recently, senior staff at the institution said that the state of the prison during the period I was staying there was a moral outrage and that children should not have been forced to live in such unhygienic conditions.

The inmates were also as hard as nails, and I knew not to act soft. I was used to adopting a tough facade. Bullying was rampant in the prison and suicides common. If an inmate's mum sent him £10, the cons would fight for it. This is where my burgeoning abilities really helped me out. I could read the auric fields around each prisoner and tell whether or not they were dangerous.

The prison population was divided among various buildings called houses. I was assigned to Hardey House, along with about a hundred other boys. Every day we were awarded association time, which meant we could gather in a large room to talk, play pool or use the phone to call home.

One day when I was on the phone talking to my mum, a lad on the phone next to me was crying his eyes out and making so much racket that I couldn't hear what Mum was saying. He looked as if he was about nineteen, and had blond hair and freckles. I thought there was something odd about him.

He had red marks around his neck.

'Help me! I need help!' The boy was hysterical.

'How can I help?' I thought, and turned away. When I turned back, he was gone. I didn't think much of it, and just went on with my conversation.

A couple of weeks later, I started to have nightmares about Freckles. Several times I heard loud sobbing.

The day following one of these nightmares, I was playing pool during association when the bell rang to signal us to return to our cells. I always lingered after the bell, trying to pinch as much leisure time as I could. I waited until one of the screws shooed me back to my cell.

'Get in there, Bolster!' The screw locked the door behind him.

I crumpled on to the bed, bored already. All of a sudden, I noticed someone was sitting in the chair by my door. It was Freckles!

'Please contact my mum,' he begged.

I almost had a heart attack. How on earth did he get into my cell? 'You need to get out of here,' I said.

As suddenly as he had appeared, he vanished. He had

looked totally real and human, but I now realized he was a ghost. Instantly, a vision flashed before me of Freckles with a strip of bed linen around his neck and then his body hanging. I screamed and yanked the emergency bell.

The screws arrived in moments, and I shouted to them that a boy had hanged himself. 'Shut up, Bolster!' a screw shouted at me. 'Loads of boys have hung themselves in here. Are you telling us you saw a ghost?' he sneered, and then whacked me in the face. They thought I was crazy and dragged me down to the punishment block, assuming I was just after attention.

They started to pummel me with their fists and, when I fell to the ground, I felt sharp kicks to my gut and back. I was afraid they would kill me but all I could do was to try and shield myself from the blows. All of a sudden, I heard a voice in my head telling me to play dead, so I made my body slump in defeat and lay totally still.

'My God! He's fuckin' dead!' The screws panicked. 'We have to get him to the hospital!'

After several minutes of feigning death, I slowly stirred and groaned in pain. They were relieved to see me alive. I lied and told them I couldn't move my back. I could see the terror in their eyes. They got a doctor to take a look at me, and he gave me some painkillers. The screws were so afraid they told me that, if I didn't tell on them, they would allow me back in a regular cell. They moved me to a different house where I didn't know anybody.

Prison was hell and that was only the beginning.

*

Once I was in the new house, I thought about Freckles and wondered why he had appeared to me. I sensed something horrible had happened to him in prison and that he had hung himself to escape the unbearable pain. All these years later, Freckles still pops into my mind and I pray that he is now at peace.

It was real torture learning the ropes in the new facility. I had to make new mates and learn again who to avoid. One screw was unusually nice to the inmates. I liked him because he treated me with respect, and we even had a few laughs together. Not long after my move, I had a vision about him. I saw him lying battered on the floor surrounded by blood.

Not a week later, I was walking out of my cell when I suddenly knew my premonition was playing itself out at that very moment. Somewhere, the kindly screw was getting kicked and stomped in the head. I ran to the staircase and saw the assault taking place on the first landing.

'Stop!' I shouted, and bounded down the steps. This was a dangerous thing to do. It was an unspoken law that inmates stood up for inmates and the screws were the enemy. I pounced on the attacker and beat the crap out of him. When it was over, I lived in fear of reprisals from the other inmates.

Retribution entered my cell in a terrifying way a few weeks later.

I was persistently tired and run-down in prison. I felt drained of energy and was constantly tapped by visions. I was also taking on the emotions of others around me. I didn't realize it then, but it depleted my own vigour and made me highly vulnerable to the spirit world.

As I now know, psychically open people like me have a bright light around them when seen from the spirit world. Spirits gather around these lights, hoping to gain a porthole to earth. That is what has happened to me throughout my life. Spirits constantly popped through my porthole because I had no idea how to police it. Now I realize that my sullen way of being opened me up to lower, darker energies.

One night at about ten o'clock I was in my cell when I sensed a malevolent energy come into the room. I couldn't move, speak, cry or scream. It felt like pure evil and I was absolutely paralysed.

Suddenly, a jug I kept on the metal shelf in the corner rose. It was as if someone invisible had picked it up. The jug flung itself around the room. I had the sense that the poltergeist, or whatever it was, had committed suicide in my cell and that he was lividly angry.

This was the first time I had felt something so malevolent. The negative entity entered my auric field and tried to link itself on to me. It took me several seconds to lose the paralysis. I screamed and leapt for the emergency bell.

The screws burst out laughing when I told them my wild story and refused to let me out of my cell. They dubbed me Spooky Joe, and this nickname spread among the convicts. The whole thing was a horrific ordeal for me. There was no way I wanted to meet up with another vile phantom like that.

*

A few months later, when I was eating dinner, I heard my name being called out.

'Spooky Joe, you've been released.' The canteen reverberated with loud claps and cheers. Apparently, the other inmates had also liked the screw who had been attacked and were glad that I had stepped in to save him. It was because I had done it that I was released. It was rare to get such a break and to have such support in the prison; usually each man was out for himself.

It was a happy day for me and I felt a new sense of hope.

Being liberated from that prison was such a relief. On my release, I travelled the three hundred miles home to Mum and Dad's house. Unfortunately, I had become hardened by then. Prison does that to you. Stealing, scams and crime were now my way of life. After a few months spent recovering from prison, I set out to make some big money.

Of course, my idea was a swindle but, if it worked, I could earn a lot of cash. I thought up a way to cheat while betting on the horse races. When you placed a bet with the bookie you had to fill in a betting slip, making a carbon copy on the sheet below, which was the part you retained. My idea was to fold the slip in half so that the name of the horse remained blank on my own chit. Later, I wrote in the name of the winning horse.

To make this work, my slip had to match the bookie's top copy, so I waited several weeks before I went to cash in. When I handed the bookie my winning slip, he paled in shock. The pay-off was £350,000! He stammered, then fumbled for the matching betting slip – but I knew it had probably already been thrown away.

When he couldn't find the slip, the bookie looked dubious, and I sensed that he had caught on to my scheme. I panicked and fled. So much for that monster money.

Undeterred, I was soon on to my next capital-raising venture. This time, I visited all the local shops and applied for credit cards. I lied about my age and wrote down a fake job. Soon my pocket was fat with credit cards. I figured that it was free money and so I moved into a flat in Beech Trees, a housing estate close to where my parents lived, and went on a whirlwind shopping spree, buying furniture, clothing, jewellery and electronic goods.

It didn't take me long to run up a debt of £9,000, but I didn't think about it until the bills arrived in the post. Of course, I was broke. I had no job, money or training. Stealing was the only life I knew.

One evening, I was awoken from my sleep by Great-uncle Tom. He was not in a dream, but standing in my room as if he were a real, living person.

'Joe, you're goin' back to jail.'

My heart sank. Sure enough, I was arrested for deception. The crown court asked if I still had any of the goods I had bought on credit. I told them yes, I had a set of velvet curtains.

The judge laughed at me. I had sold all the other things to get my hands on some cash. I had even taken orders, so people had paid me to buy specific items, such as televisions or VCRs. The judge sentenced me to twenty-one months in prison.

I was hauled to HM Prison, Risley, which was fifty miles from Skelmersdale. It was considered one of the nastiest prisons in the country. I immediately tapped into visions of men hanging themselves, of beatings and real savagery. The prison was a virtual gang, and the screws did not hesitate to use brute force on the inmates. Because of the degree of bullying, a lot of lads committed suicide.

There was a man there called Mick the Dog, and I had a premonition that he would fall off a motorbike and die. It was another premonition that would turn out to be true. I read about the accident in the paper a few years later.

One day, I kept hearing a voice in my cell: 'You can raise your energy if you say these words – "Enhance psychic ability."' I started shouting those words over and over until the screws came and moved me to an isolation cell in the block.

I was so bored there that I cooked up a scheme with the other inmates in isolation. The walls of the cells were made of brick, and I told the prisoners that if they knocked away at them we would eventually meet halfway through. I used my heavy metal bed to bang on my wall. It was highly amusing, but stupid, of course.

The noise we made must have sounded like a prison revolt, because the next thing I knew, some screws burst into my cell in full riot gear – helmets and shields, the lot – wielding batons. I was beaten severely and dragged into a strip cell where they tore off my clothes. They wrestled me into a straitjacket and dumped me in a secluded cell.

Talk about misery. Cockroaches and mice crawled over my naked skin – and I was petrified of rodents and insects. Being locked up like that, among paedophiles and other scum of the earth, was the worst experience of my life. All I could hear was the screaming from the other cells as inmates thrashed out their demons and tried to keep clear of the vermin.

A couple of weeks later, I was saved by my twenty-first birthday. I was now legally an adult. I was moved to the adult section of the prison and placed in isolation to assist my transition. However, my feelings of relief didn't last long. The adult block was even worse than the juvenile section, and housed hardened criminals, drug dealers and murderous gangsters. One guy accidentally shot his friend's head off.

I had to act tough, and to help I worked out daily in my cell, doing push-ups and other exercises to stay fit. There was one screw from Scotland who tried to be kind and compassionate, even offering me puffs of his cigar. I didn't like smoking but considered his offer a privilege and therefore not something to be turned down.

One day, I had a vision of myself fighting with another screw. The scene switched to guards in riot gear. I now trusted my premonitions and I didn't want this vision to come true. I understood that the screws were capable of violence on an inhuman scale and decided to avoid conflict and stop the vision from becoming reality.

The living conditions in the jail were deplorable. We

were only allowed out of our cells for five minutes a day, to wash and use the toilet. Each cell had a bucket if we needed it during the day. This meant we had to smell the contents all day and slop out in the five-minute break.

Once, while I was using a small hand mirror to have a quick shave during the break, a screw opened the door and demanded that I give him it. I was furious. The mirror had been issued to me by the prison, and it seemed unfair for him to confiscate it. As he reached for it, I jerked it away. An argument ensued, and the screw kicked me in the shins with full force.

I doubled over in pain. It seemed so pointless and cruel. I grabbed the screw by his hair and dragged him into the cell. I told him not to kick me again. Then I remembered the vision and changed my tone. I was ordered to face the governor for further punishment.

'What is your number?' the governor asked.

I was so angry that they were chastising me for an incident that the screw had provoked that I couldn't stop myself from spitting, 'Piss off!' at him.

The governor went mad. 'What is your number?' he demanded again.

I saw the screw who shared his cigar with me chuckle. I think he was proud of me for standing my ground. It didn't help, though. I was hauled out of there and screws in riot gear attacked me. The vision I had experienced played itself out, and they stripped me down, stuffed me into a straitjacket and dumped me in the isolation block.

I went into meltdown and suffered severe depression. A doctor was sent to check up on me every day.

'Are you okay?' he would ask, genuinely concerned.

'Do I fuckin' look okay?' I snapped.

Because I was so aggressive, the doctor kept me in the straitjacket, which only fuelled my rage further. I lay there in a heap of misery when, suddenly, Great-uncle Tom appeared.

'Tell the doctor you're fine.'

I was so grateful to see a friendly face, and it made me realize that I was only making my situation worse with my attitude. The next day, when the doctor asked how I was feeling, I replied, 'I haven't felt this good in years!' It worked. He released me from the straitjacket.

I vowed then and there to follow my great-uncle's advice from then on but, sadly, it wasn't a vow that I would keep.

When I was finally released from isolation, I was shipped me off to Walton Prison. If I'd thought it couldn't be worse than Risley, I was soon proved wrong. They kept me in the seclusion block for a few days, I suppose as a transition before moving into what turned out to be pure hell – as if I hadn't already seen enough brutality in prison. In Walton, because of overcrowding, the paedophiles and the hardest criminals were mixed in with the regular prison population.

In prison, paedophiles are considered the lowest of the low. Both the inmates and the guards hate them and, in Walton, the screws would even tip off the prisoners when a child molester was moved to the main landings, so the inmates would assault them. It happened on a regular basis, and the beatings were downright savage. The inmates would hide large radio batteries inside socks and use them as weapons.

One day, I was standing outside my cell when I saw a gigantic black man with bulging muscles. I could see a dirty red aura surrounding him, and I saw him beating his wife and stabbing a white man to death. I knew he was vile, but I couldn't help staring at his aura.

The next day, he grabbed me by the neck and dragged me into his cell.

'What were you fuckin' lookin' at?' he roared.

'Nothin'. Just wonderin' what you're in here for.'

He still had me by the neck, and I could feel my eyes bulging. 'Don't you ever fuckin' ask me anything or I'll kill you!'

I was scared he'd strangle me, but he let go and shoved me out of his cell. I never looked his way again.

After what seemed like much longer, my twenty-one-month sentence finally ended. My experiences in prison had taught me that I never wanted to go back. I had no idea how I would do it, but I drew the line and decided that I wanted to change my ways. I no longer wanted a life of crime, violence and prison.

7

I was twenty-two years old when I got out of prison, and they handed me a £200 grant to get me on my feet again. It wasn't much, but I was determined to earn money honestly this time.

My mate Tony Ollie and I pooled our cash and took £450 to the bulk warehouse in Manchester. Chino trousers were all the rage back in the 1980s, so we bought a load, and various toys, and sold them in our local pubs. We let our customers pay on tick, jacking up the prices to make the instalments sound cheaper. Within a few weeks, we had made a tidy profit of £1,000.

Christmas was approaching, so Ollie and I decided to invest our earnings in children's toys. We stocked up at the warehouse and sold them on tick, too. It didn't take long for people to realize we were overcharging and that the same toys were sold more cheaply in the shops. It was the simple rule of business: the big stores bought in huge quantities and got a better price wholesale, and so were able to sell for less. I realized we didn't have a chance against the larger shops, so I shut down that particular enterprise.

The following summer, I was strolling around the Southport fairgrounds with Quinny, the mate who had had the scare with the Ouija board, and his girlfriend,

Diane. The fair was loaded with fortune-tellers and gypsies, who looked into their crystal balls and supposedly read your future. Diane suggested we go for a reading. Quinny and I were against it, but we followed Diane to join a long queue, where one particular gypsy woman was charging a mighty £6 for a reading. Diane went in first, while Quinny and I waited outside.

'She was great,' Diane gushed when she came out. 'She told me to get rid of my boyfriend.'

Quinny's face fell, but Diane chuckled. After that sour advice, Quinny refused to see the gypsy, so I went inside. When I took my seat across from the woman, I was totally sceptical, but she unnerved me, staring right through me as if she could see into my very soul. Ready to flee, my feet started dancing.

'I've been waiting for you a long time,' she said earnestly.

That was freaky, but I was certain she was a typical con.

'You've been staying in a mate's flat. It's painted lime green at the top of the landing.'

I pricked up my ears at that. Her description of the horrid green paint was totally accurate.

'You drive a red car.'

Right again! Now she really had my attention.

She fiddled with some cards, but I knew she didn't need them. I could see a man standing behind her and knew it was her spirit guide, feeding her the information.

'Be careful of a dark-haired woman,' she said, and fell into a trance. It lasted a long time, which frightened me a little.

'You fall under her spell. I see children, and you're going on a journey to prison.'

Goosebumps rose all over my body. I could not imagine going to prison again and was determined to stay away from crime. Her prediction could not come true.

'I see drugs, drugs, drugs . . . lots of drugs.'

At this, I felt somewhat relieved because, despite all my illegal activity in the past, I had never been involved with drugs. Once, when I was younger, I had tried smoking pot, but it made me sick. I thought of Quinny, who did smoke marijuana. Maybe this prediction was for him. He was, after all, standing right outside. I was sure the drugs and prison forecasts were incorrect.

'Now I'm seeing television.'

That was a real puzzle. Would I be on TV because of drugs? It didn't make sense.

'That is all for now,' she said, shaking herself back into the present. 'You will need to come back later for more.'

When I told Quinny about the predictions, he half smiled. 'I know I won't go to prison for drugs,' I asserted. 'She must be wrong about that.'

I quickly forgot about the gypsy's predictions and went about my new life, setting up house, once again in Beech Trees. I was friendly with my neighbours, Liz and Mike Newberry, who had a young son named James. The little boy had a sickly auric field, and I learned he suffered from cystic fibrosis. In a flash vision I saw he that he would die but, as Liz and Mike were good friends, I didn't have the heart to tell them.

One night, I met an intriguing woman when I was out clubbing. Her name was Pippa and she was nine years older than me and had two children. I should have been wary when she told me she was separated from her husband because he was mixed up in drugs. She also had short dark hair. However, the gypsy's prediction forgotten, I jumped feet first into a relationship with her.

While I was dating Pippa, I bought and sold cars to make money. I managed to save a little bit and bought a big old box van for £150 and set it up in the little square where I lived.

I used the van to open a mobile shop, from which I sold food and cigarettes. It caught on quickly, because I was good to my customers, letting them pay at the end of the week or when they got their pay cheque. I built up the business, catering to my customers, and felt proud to be earning an honest living.

Soon after I met Pippa, she announced that she was pregnant. I was thrilled and immediately had a vision.

'The baby is a boy,' I told her.

'How do you know?'

'I just know. We must call him Joseph, after me.'

Sure enough, little Joseph was born in 1990, when I was twenty-three. With my baby son I was happier than I had ever been. My business was flourishing, and money was flowing from a legal source. Pippa and I bought nice furniture and decorated our house. It was a happy time. Soon, Pippa was pregnant again and this time I knew it was a girl. Maria was born in 1992.

Not long afterwards I opened up a second mobile shop in a nearby housing estate called Carfield. I was finally getting my life in order, and I adored three-year-old Joseph, and Maria, who was only nine months old.

At around about the same time, the newspaper headlines blazed with news of a massive drugs bust in Skelmersdale. The articles said that police had confiscated £100,000 worth of drugs from a garden shed at Chris Sanders' house. Chris was a mate of my brother, Johnny. In fact, many of my brother's friends had been arrested in the drugs raid.

I was lying on the couch one evening when, all of a sudden, I heard somebody pounding on the door. My heart just about exploded when the door crashed in and at least fifteen police officers burst into the house. I freaked out at the intensity of the raid, afraid it would upset my children. The cops told me I was under arrest for trafficking drugs. I was horrified, as I had been living an honest life since I had been released from prison. It was like one of those police shows, where they bust in and arrest the big drug kingpin. I was handcuffed and thrown into a police van.

I knew it was a big mistake. Surely the police would free me when they didn't find drugs on me or in my house? I was completely innocent. The truth would prevail and I would be released. Imagine my shock when bail was refused and I was remanded in custody.

I was frightened out of my mind as I sat in the cell trying to figure out why they thought I was involved with drugs. I wondered if my brother's friends had lied about me to take the heat off themselves.

I hired a barrister to represent me; she would handle my case in the crown court. She was a very diligent lawyer and learned that the evidence against me was my two mobile shops, the fact that I had money and nice home furnishings. The police reckoned everything had been bought with drugs money. My barrister was shocked, but the police went ahead and built a case around this assumption.

I was outraged. I had earned that money honestly. I was proud of the new life I had worked hard to create, and it ripped my heart out for the police to make a mockery of all my efforts.

My barrister persisted in trying to find out why I had been arrested. It was ludicrous – there was no evidence against me. The authorities were downright corrupt, and told my barrister and the judge that they had secret proof which they could not share until the trial because it would damage the case against the others. They explained that they would not release me because I could interfere with other witnesses' testimony.

While I was stuck in jail, my neighbour Fiona brought the kids to see me. She told me that Pippa had begun a relationship with another man. I felt totally beaten down and had a sort of breakdown in jail. Why did this have to happen to me, just when I was trying to go straight?

My barrister fought heart and soul to get me out of jail; she just couldn't figure out why I was there. I was facing up to ten years in prison. She had to appoint a Queen's

Counsel. On the day of my trial, emotions ran high in the crown court, where I was offered a plea deal.

'If you plead guilty, your sentence will be reduced to seven years.'

I was also told that if I did not plead guilty I would lose at trial and spend ten years in prison. I couldn't bring myself to plead guilty, but there was also no way I could ever spend any more time in prison. I agreed to sign the guilty plea but also insisted that I sign a note that declared that I did not commit the crime. It was the smartest thing I have ever done in my life.

Soon afterwards, the police realized that they had no evidence against me. They didn't want to be charged with wrongful arrest, so they released me, saying it was because I had signed the paper saying I was innocent.

I was relieved to be out of prison, but my body was physically shattered. And the pleasant life I had created for myself had been destroyed, too. I had no girlfriend, no house and no possessions.

My situation was dismal.

It was time to go back and see the gypsy.

I returned to Southport fairground on a mission. I peeped through the curtain to make sure the fortune-teller I had seen before was there. It was her, and I felt the same odd feelings about her when I entered the room. I didn't think she would recognize me as I had cut my long, curly hair short.

She barely looked at me and shuffled a deck of Tarot cards as I took a seat. 'You've been here before.' She seemed to recognize my energy more than my face. She laid out some cards on the table and pointed to one. 'This is the death card,' she declared.

Then she was silent. I stared at the card, longing to run away.

'You ignored my advice,' she said. 'You've been through a rough time with prison and relationships.' She flipped more cards on to the table and studied them. 'You have a son and a daughter. I see the initials J and M.'

She was startlingly accurate.

She turned up several more cards, as if she were gazing into my future. 'I see more troubled times ahead.'

I froze. 'Am I going to die?' I blurted out. I didn't know anything about Tarot cards at that time, and the death card terrified me.

'The death card means an ending inside of you, not your physical death. In other words, an emptiness inside you will transform into fulfilment. There really are great times ahead. But you face more struggles before the pathway clears. You must avoid greed. It's time to bring out your true gifts.'

I liked the idea of a positive breakthrough, but I was frightened at the thought of there being more difficulties ahead.

'Don't be afraid,' she told me. 'I know you are confused by this, but you will eventually understand everything. It will all be revealed at a later date. I am not allowed to pass it along.' Then she shouted, 'Enough! Pass me your hands.' She grasped my wrists. I watched her eyes roll back, and she entered a trance-like state.

'I see an accident.' She hesitated, as if she were studying the scene. 'It's too late! But you'll be okay.' She remained in her mind, still clutching my wrists. 'Your life is about to make a U-turn ... 180 degrees. I see fire! Fire! Fire! A house blaze.' She fell into a fit, shaking.

This really freaked me out, because I had seen several visions of my young neighbour James Newberry, the one with cystic fibrosis, passing into the spirit world. Did this warning have something to do with him?

The gypsy shrieked, making a sound that could have come straight out of *The Exorcist*. Once again, her eyes rolled back, and she screamed, 'The gun! The gun! Avoid the gun!'

I jerked my hands away, tossed £10 on the table and ran out.

After my trip to see the gypsy fortune-teller, I had a series of nightmares in which I saw myself lying in a pool of blood, my face also bleeding profusely. The horrifying dreams persisted. I dreaded another round of trouble, as the gypsy had predicted.

I was still depressed over what had happened with Pippa and wasn't thrilled when a good friend of mine, Kelly, started dating a man from a family that had a bit of a reputation for being tough and did not see eye to eye with the Bolsters. They had a lot of respect locally because they oozed money and owned a pub called the Night Owl. Kelly's boyfriend, Jack Caine, had two brothers who often got into scuffles with our brother Denny.

One night, I was heading out to the Night Owl when

Great-uncle Tom appeared. 'Do not go!' he commanded.

I was in the habit of ignoring him and, even though he repeated his warning while I was getting ready to go, I felt I needed a night out of my dreary flat.

I met up with some mates at the pub and we were having a laugh. I happened to glance up the steps and saw Denny arguing loudly with Jack's brother, Leo. I sensed Denny was in danger so I hot-tailed it up the stairs.

Jack was watching the whole thing, and must have thought I was going to attack Leo. He charged at me and bit my nose. He had my entire nose in his mouth when the Caines' uncle jumped in and kicked me in the head. My nose was ripped off by the force of it and was now hanging on to my face by a few shreds of skin.

Blood spurted everywhere. The Caines ran and, like a raving lunatic, I lumbered after them, blood pouring down my face. The next thing I remember is people holding me and being loaded into an ambulance. The doctors sewed my nose back on, but the injury was so severe that I had to have skin grafts. You can still see the scars today.

I realized that the gypsy had been right about there being more trouble ahead. I was also angry that I hadn't taken any notice of my great-uncle's warning. When would I learn? And what made the whole thing even more gutting was that the Caines got away with it. It was an unwritten rule that gang members never called the police to grass on each other.

I was furious, but there was no way I would ever be called a grass.

*

After that incident, I felt even lower, physically, emotionally and spiritually. I sank into a heavy depression, not helped by the fact that I was now on the dole. I scraped by and lived on the government's ration of £40 a week.

The flat I lived in was a dismal place. I had a vision that the man upstairs had committed suicide and, sure enough, when I returned from a trip to Wales, I learned that he had hanged himself. The vision told me he had been estranged from his parents, which had devastated him.

I sat in pubs and had premonitions there, too. My mind saw a man running up the steps of our complex with a Stanley knife and cutting a woman's face. It happened in reality just a few weeks later.

I was unemployed for quite a few months and was sick and tired of my miserable life. One day, I had flopped in desolation on a chair in my flat. My body felt like lead, and I was wallowing in self-pity. Suddenly, a grey mist or haze started to appear and, soon, it suffused the room. The atmosphere changed from being pitiful to being loving. I recognized a tremendous, warm energy, and a feeling of exhilaration swept over me. Then, a few seconds later, two Chinese people appeared before me. They were elderly and communicated through their consciousnesses that they were Mr and Mrs Deng, my spirit parents. This was really confusing. Parents? I already had parents on the earth, and these people were Chinese. Yet I sensed a strong connection with and affection towards them.

I felt a jolt and, the next thing I knew, I was out of

my body and following the Dengs on a journey. I flowed easily with the energy through a maze of sights. We floated over rolling hills and grassy fields. The Dengs showed me a vision of them hard at work in China. I saw their lives play out from their younger days on earth right through to reaching old age. We finally stopped at an ancient Chinese building with weathered doors. They led me through the first door and I saw myself lying there, sullen. The atmosphere was dark and gloomy, and I realized it was a space of no opportunity. The Dengs explained that this room showed my current predicament.

'You are in danger, Joe,' Mr Deng said. 'You are not doing what you came to earth to do.'

This frightened me, as I knew that I was wasting my life, floundering about in my depressed torpor. The more I studied the room, the more I realized that, if I continued on this path, I would die early. It worried me.

The Dengs guided me through a brighter door and, inside, I saw changing images of various teachers and higher education. I saw these spirit educators working with various earthlings to impart knowledge from the spirit side. These teachers are the source of the bright ideas which suddenly pop into our minds on earth. They conveyed wisdom and insight with a tender whisper. The earthlings had no idea that these wise sages were giving them such immense guidance. This room was showing me that I had a choice: I could waste my life away or tap into the spiritual guidance that is available to everyone.

'You came to the earth with a strong purpose,' Mrs

Deng said. 'It's ready to fall apart unless you make some changes. You are on the earth to help people.'

Why? I asked through my consciousness.

'It will appear to you.'

Abruptly, I was back in my flat. I sat in shock, reeling at the powerful journey I had been taken on and thoroughly intrigued by what I had seen in the spirit realm. Who were these spirit parents? What could I give to help others? I felt as if I had been sleepwalking all my life.

Two days later, the Dengs visited again. I was so happy to see them and learn more. They continued to come for many weeks, and I looked forward to their visits. They always arrived with the grey mist; the TV or radio would crackle and the neighbour's dog would bark like crazy.

They shared much more about spiritual guides and teachers with me. They also showed me around the spirit world, offering insight into what happens when one commits suicide and where we go when we die. I found it all fascinating.

They finally touched on my true purpose on earth. I hadn't known at the time that the strange visions, voices and experiences I had had throughout my entire life were all part of my reason for living.

All of this lifted my mood, and I took a few small building jobs, such as plastering or painting. I hated physical labour, though, and I was never good at it. Even after my visits with the Dengs, my mind was on making money in sales, where I knew I had talent.

At the time, I had no idea that what the Dengs were

teaching me was my true life mission, but looking back, I can see how important it was.

Soon after my first visit from the Dengs, the Caine family barred Denny from the Night Owl, because Jack's two brothers hated him. But Denny wouldn't have cared if the Caines had been members of the Mafia; he wasn't going to be intimidated by their reputation.

Denny was a bubbly, witty fellow who enjoyed his own company, but he was into heroin. It was that, and his bravado, that led him to the Night Owl one night. Once there, he slipped into a corner booth so the Caines wouldn't see him. I had decided to go that night, too, with my other brother, Johnny, but Great-uncle Tom and Auntie Emmie immediately popped in and warned me not to. I really should have learned to take their advice by that point, but I went anyway.

I was sitting in the pub talking to Johnny when I heard a huge commotion upstairs. Call it intuition, but I bounded up the steps, and found Leo aiming a gun at Denny. I had no time to think. I whacked Leo's face with such force he dropped the gun.

Silence.

It was now all about two rival families from two opposing gangs. Leo was highly respected in the criminal fraternity, and didn't want to lose face in front of his entire family. The place exploded in mayhem. The family went berserk. Johnny had two mates who were up for a fight. Rory was six-foot-seven and built like a brick shithouse. His pal, Ringo, had just got out of prison for murder. They put me up against Leo in a one-on-one fight.

The doors were shut and locked so that nobody could leave. Rory, Ringo and the owners created a ring where I would fight Leo. It was to be a fist fight, and Leo slugged me first, in the head. I was seeing stars, but I knew in my gut that I couldn't lose this fight. It was one of the toughest fights I've ever been in. In the end Leo backed down because he was black and blue. I had barely a scratch.

I wasn't proud of fighting. I knew the Caines had been justified in kicking Denny out of their pub. I learned later that the owner, Timmy, had seen Denny in the Night Owl and asked him to leave.

'I'm gonna finish my pint,' Denny had said, bolshily. He had also been disrespectful to Timmy's father, Larry. I could understand that they were angry – but pulling a gun was preposterous.

The gypsy's warning – 'The gun!' – echoed in my mind.

Several weeks later, Great-uncle Tom told me to be very careful wherever I went. I dismissed his warning, thinking he must have been referring to the bar fight. But his warnings grew stronger over the next few months, and I began to be frightened that someone would shoot me.

One day, I was in Bournemouth and ran into a guy named Delmol, who was a well-known figure in the underworld. He was best friends with Leo. 'Joe, he hired a hit man to kill you!' Delmol said. 'You shamed the Caines, so they have a hit out on you.'

I was terrified, and now I began to take heed of my dream warnings. I was careful getting in and out of cars and when leaving my house. Was I grateful when Delmol insisted that Leo call off the hit man!

But still, I had no real idea if the Caines had finally called off any plan of revenge.

8

As if I didn't have enough problems at the time, I began to have a series of dreams and visions that sent me into a total panic. My daughter Maria was five in 1997 and, in these dreams, she was in danger. As the visions developed, I visualized her in an accident and warned Pippa always to buckle her into a seatbelt when she put her in the car. The dreams eventually revealed that I would be in the accident with Maria.

One day, my sister Diane was visiting from her home in Cyprus. Maria was staying with me that day, and I was having a bit of trouble with the police. I had been pulled over while driving and I didn't have the necessary documents on me, such as proof of insurance or the MOT certificate. The police had told me to take the papers along to Wigan police station in the next few days.

At that time, Maria was a daddy's girl. She would cling to me like a wet bathing suit, so I asked if she wanted to go with me to the police station.

Her little face lit up, then I saw it melt into a frown. 'No, Dad, I'd better stay here with Auntie Diane.'

Both Diane and I were surprised. 'Are you okay, Maria?' I asked her. I could tell from her dubious expression that she did not know herself why she was turning down a trip with Daddy.

'Okay, I'm on my way.' I jumped into the car and headed to Wigan. While I was driving, I thought about why Maria hadn't wanted to come. Had a spirit friend whispered something in her ear? I started to cross a narrow bridge and, suddenly, I saw a car heading straight towards me. It hit me head on.

I remember the impact, then I was instantly out of my body, travelling to a place suffused with bright light. Priests in long robes and other spiritual guides wearing gowns stood scattered about. Then I was sitting on a bench next to a row of other people. Was I dead? One of the gowned men was summoning those ahead of me on the bench. I realized I was waiting my turn.

When he finally came to me, he said, 'It is not your time yet. You must go back.'

I jolted back into my aching body, which was slumped in my smashed car. A woman dragged me out of the wreckage and tried to communicate with me. I was more interested in the spirit people around me. I felt at peace with them. I knew intuitively that I was on a fine line between life and crossing over.

My head was pounding, and I realized that I had smashed the right side of it on the post by the side window. Blood poured from the wound. People were trying to staunch the bleeding with whatever material they had to hand.

'You will be okay,' a spirit visitor said.

That message was soothing, but I was still frightened in the ambulance that rushed me to hospital. The damage was severe. The right side of my head had been bashed in, and the doctor had to repair it with skin grafts. I spent nine days in the hospital and, for many years afterwards, I had small seizures and was unsteady on my feet. I often fell down while I was just walking along.

The accident rattled me for a long time, but I was always grateful that my precious Maria had turned down a ride with her dad that day. The side of the car she would have been in was a write-off. There was no way she would have survived.

To this day, I am convinced that I did die that day but for some reason I was ordered back to fulfil some kind of a mission. I was thirty years old and had no idea what that mission might be.

While I was recovering from the accident, I moved to a flat in Ormskirk. I began to have lots of visions and insights that someone in my family was going to die. I bought some Tarot cards, desperately trying to work it out. I saw a funeral in our family and, because my father was always ill, I figured it was him that would die. I even contacted the insurance company to make sure he was covered.

The person I glimpsed in the casket had curly hair like Dad's. I was terrified but, again, I didn't tell anyone about these visions. I had these premonitions for two years. During that time, my friend Fiona moved to Bournemouth, and I visited her frequently. It was a great place for me to stay, and my children could visit me easily. One night when I was sleeping on Fiona's couch in Bournemouth, the vision of a woman came to me in my sleep.

She said her name was Alexandra Pistonie, and that she used to be a nun on earth. She told me that Fiona had applied to receive welfare benefits but had been refused. Fiona had appealed, and Alexandra said that the appeal had been successful and that the money would arrive soon. I had no idea that Fiona, who had five children, had applied for government assistance.

When I woke up, Fiona was getting the kids ready for school. I told her that she had won her appeal and that the money would come through shortly. Of course, she was surprised, as she knew I had had no idea that she had applied for benefits in the first place. Sure enough, at 9.30 that morning, a cheque arrived in the post.

I was still trying to recover, physically and mentally, from the accident. I could barely walk out of the door without falling over. I lost my confidence. I was in and out of hospitals as doctors tried out various treatments and drugs. They gave me pills for epilepsy, but I sensed that that wasn't what was wrong with me, so I didn't take them. It was a very harrowing time.

Finally, a specialist worked out what the problem was. My sense of balance had been permanently damaged in the accident. He put me on some different medication and I felt like a new person. I still take the pills if I feel unstable on my feet. It was heaven to feel normal again.

During that traumatic time, my brother Denny told me that he sensed he was going to die. I realized he was highly sensitive and intuitive. He begged me to read his palm for him. 'I know I'm not going to live,' he told me.

'Why do you want me to read your palm?' I asked. Even with all the psychic experiences I had had, I did not consider myself to be a psychic. But Denny had curly hair, and the premonitions I was having were clear about it being a curly-haired family member in a coffin.

I had a hard time understanding Denny's insight. I loved my brother, whom I considered fun-loving, intelligent and witty. We were very close. He wasn't depressed. He was making this prediction with all his faculties intact. He wasn't morbid, but I realized he had a serious insight into his future. He went to see a fortune-teller, Sue, even though I warned him against it. Sue confirmed that he would die. Denny, as you can imagine, was horrified, and so was I.

'Don't believe her,' I insisted. 'If you trust in what she said, you could bring it on with your thoughts.' Inside, I was furious with Sue.

Mum had always had a sixth sense about Denny, especially that time he was seriously ill with meningitis. She also knew, and was worried, about him using heroin. Denny was a decent fellow – he didn't rob or steal for money, he earned it legitimately, but he spent a lot on heroin. In order to keep him out of danger, Mum persuaded him to go and live in Cyprus, near my sister Diane.

Denny lived and thrived in Cyprus for fifteen months. When he came back, he was off drugs, working and looked brilliant. We were thrilled for him. But the streets of Skelmersdale were flooded with heroin, crack, cocaine and crystal meth. Denny met up with his old mates, and his old habits kicked in again. He went back on heroin. It seemed as if he was fighting a losing battle. He broke up with his girlfriend and became separated from his three children.

Mum tried to help him and asked me if Denny could move into my flat for a while. I kept a small lovebird parrot at the time and the moment Denny walked into my flat, it dropped dead. I immediately remembered the time Denny had thrown the dead bird into our Indian neighbours' house. They had said that, in India, a dead bird represents death in the family. Was this an omen for Denny?

The following week, I again drove the three hundred miles back to Bournemouth to see the kids and stay with Fiona. At about nine that evening, we were talking in the living room. Across from us was a set of glass doors. I glanced over and saw the number seven drawn in red paint on the right door.

'Look at that number seven,' Fiona declared, pointing at the door. We both saw it. Fiona bounced up and closed the curtains, thinking it might be a reflection on the glass. But the number was strong and clear on the door.

'Seven deadly sins,' Fiona said.

'Piss off!' I snapped back. It made no sense, and I was not in the mood to listen to stupid remarks. But maybe a spirit was whispering in her ear. It was a powerful and unusual thing for Fiona to say. She went to bed, and I went to sleep on the couch.

In my sleep, I saw a man and woman standing behind me. In my gut, I knew I was going on a journey to a forbidden place. I was fighting not to go.

'It is a sacred place,' the woman said. 'This is only for people who have passed over.'

I felt a strong certainty that it was not my time to die but that these people were offering me a huge insight into the afterlife. I lost my fight not to go with them and found myself travelling at lightning speed on an OBE journey. I had never travelled so quickly before.

Soon, I was standing in front of an old marketplace. Everything about it was just as it would be if it had been a marketplace on earth, with people ambling about, doing their normal shopping. I heard a man's voice, which was very familiar to me but I couldn't quite place it.

'I'm all right here. I'm okay, and I'm safe.' A warm, loving energy blanketed me, and I felt peaceful and content. I had never felt this degree or quality of comfort before. I still couldn't put my finger on the owner of the voice.

In a sudden flash, I was told that all the people in the marketplace were dead. All had lived on the earth but had passed into eternal life. It looked just like our earth life. I saw quick bursts of people living, and spirits, but the main message came from that male voice saying that he was okay.

'It is not your time,' my female guide said. 'You are not supposed to experience the other side. This was a special gift.'

I was probably on my journey for only two minutes,

but it seemed much longer. I jerked back into my body and woke up. I was so disturbed by what I had experienced that I lay awake for the rest of the night.

The next day, I told Fiona about my travels. I felt great all day, with a peace and tranquillity that had eluded me for years.

At about five o'clock that evening, the phone rang. It was James Newberry, my neighbour, the one who suffered from cystic fibrosis. 'I have something to tell you, but I can't,' he stammered.

My heart leaped. 'Is it about Denny?'

'Yes. He's dead.'

My dream came flooding back to me, and I now recognized that the voice in the spiritual marketplace had been Denny's. He was on the other side, and he had said he was okay. I drove the five hours back to Skelmersdale in a state of shock.

At Mum's house, the story spilled out. Mum said that, a week before Denny died, he had told her people were out to kill him. Mum didn't know why, but she had asked what she could do to help.

'It's too late,' he told her. 'They're after me. I'm going to get away and hide.'

Unfortunately, Mum thought he was exaggerating because he was involved with drugs. We learned that Denny had been hanging out getting high on heroin with Richie Wood and May Christie who were half-siblings, sharing the same father. It was well known among Denny's friends that he never injected drugs. But Richie and May did.

Mum had been concerned when Denny hadn't come round for a few days. She sent the younger kids over to Denny's house to make sure he was all right. My younger sister, Louise, looked through the window but didn't see anything. Finally, the window cleaner kicked in the door and found Denny's body. 'Don't come in here!' he warned Louise. Denny's body was on the bed, and he held a syringe in his right hand. The post-mortem report showed that he had enough heroin in his system to kill an elephant. He would have died instantly. It was the report's opinion that it was a fatal overdose.

But something didn't add up. Denny was left-handed, but the syringe was in his right hand. And if the huge injection of heroin had killed him instantly, and he had administered the injection himself, wouldn't the needle still be in his arm, rather than his hand?

Two days after Denny's body was found, I had a spirit visitation from Great-uncle Tom, and this time my Auntie Emmie came along. She had been the psychic of the family, and it was great to see her. They told me to go to Denny's house, which I did immediately.

I talked to his neighbour, Angela, who told me that three blokes had knocked on Denny's door the Saturday before his body was found. Denny had sneaked over to Angela's and used the phone to call the police. The call is documented in police reports.

Inside Denny's house, I was horrified to find knives stacked in the sink. Denny must have been terrified that someone was after him. In the bedroom, I found a suit-case with clothes packed. Great-uncle Tom appeared and told me to examine the carpet. I found a large patch of body fluids on the carpet, about five feet from the bed. It was obvious someone had moved Denny's body. This was no accident.

I learned that Richie Wood had bragged to a friend named Les Cassin and his wife, Patricia, that he had been paid to kill Denny Bolster. Les and Patricia went to the police and reported what Richie had told them. The CID took statements, which are still on file. They maintain that Denny was murdered on Sunday. His body was discovered on Wednesday, *after* my dream of meeting him in the afterlife.

A few days after Denny's death, I cornered May Christie and asked her what had happened to Denny. She burst into tears. 'I can't tell you,' she cried.

I had a sudden flash of May dying. 'That's not good enough,' I shouted. 'He was my brother.' I gave her my phone number, which wasn't listed. 'When you're ready to tell me more, call me.'

An hour later, my phone rang. 'Is Denny there?' a man's voice asked.

I froze, but played along. 'He's not here. He'll be back in a few hours,' I lied. I knew what the call meant. It was a warning to lay off May.

Richie Wood was arrested, but the two statements were not enough to hold him in custody. Richie also had an alibi – he had been in hospital awaiting surgery. Friends, however, later said that they had bought drugs from him on that date, so he was not in hospital for the entire day. His mother tried to cover for him by stopping by at Mum's house and offering her condolences. Nine months later, May died of a heroin overdose.

Denny's slaying was a shocking loss for our family. No one was ever charged with his murder. At his grave, I stared at the headstone: 7 March 1999. There was that seven that Fiona and I had seen spiritually painted in red. Oddly, every address I lived at as an adult added up to seven. My house number at that time was forty-three.

My parents were devastated when Denny died, and felt they needed to get away, so a few weeks afterwards they went to visit my sister in Cyprus. They asked me to stay at their house with my youngest brother, Peter, who was frightened after all the turmoil.

I slept on the couch, with Peter next to me. The first night, I had a vivid dream. I was standing in my flat and the front door was wide open. A woman appeared at the entrance. I recognized my Great-aunt Emmie again, who looked just like any other living human being. Her gaze cut through me and went straight to my soul.

'I've been with you through all the mayhem,' she said. 'I met Denny when he arrived on this side. Joe, you're very clairvoyant.'

I saw a quick flash of my future, then a hulking man of about six-foot-five walked towards me. I didn't recognize his energy and jumped back in fear. Was he going to come to get me in the future?

A loud gong sounded, and I jerked awake. I was facing Mum's grandfather clock, which was chiming seven. There was that seven again. It scared me. I lay there for a while, staring at the clock. The dream and the timely awakening had given me a fright.

The next day, I visited my Uncle Terry and told him about the spirit visit from Great-aunt Emmie. I described the lofty man, and Terry nodded. 'That must be your Great-great-uncle Jack.'

I felt better hearing that. If it was a great-great-uncle, at least it wasn't a warning that I was about to have a serious run-in with a six-foot-five bruiser.

A few weeks later, my sister Maria asked me to attend a session at a Skelmersdale spiritualist church. I had absolutely no interest in religion, but Maria kept on at me, saying that it wasn't like a regular church. Maria worked at a pub and said she had never attended this spiritual service either. She told me a medium would conduct readings there. As I knew Maria was generally sceptical about things like that, I thought it was odd she was so adamant about giving this a try.

I finally caved in, and Maria and I went together and sat in the front row. The medium quickly homed in on my sister, but Maria was cynical about the message she was given. 'I have no idea what you're talking about,' she said to the medium.

'The man next to you is your brother,' the medium offered. 'You have recently lost a young man.' At this, we both sat up in our chairs. The medium turned to me. 'I have a gentleman in spirit who wants to talk. He says he was a professional boxer and died of cancer.'

I huffed. I wanted to talk with Denny, not some other

dead guy I didn't even know. Boxer? Cancer? It made no sense. 'No, that visitor is not for me,' I said.

'I have been doing this work for thirty-seven years,' the medium continued. 'You are a natural medium. You are meant to do this professionally, and you will be at it for a long time.'

That was the last thing I wanted to hear. I would have preferred to converse with my dead brother.

'Go home and think about it overnight,' the medium said.

I must say, I was a bit perturbed after this reading. But before Maria and I left the church, someone tapped me on the shoulder. 'I'll see you next week,' I heard a man say. I turned around, but there was nobody there.

Back in my flat, I did think about the medium's prediction, although it still didn't really inspire me. I thought he was just charming me, since he had been wrong about the boxer wanting to talk to me. Despite my lifelong experience of psychic occurrences, being a medium held no interest or intrigue for me.

I slept at Mum's that night, and the next morning I remembered Denny's friend Jimmy, who had died of cancer about a week before Denny's death. He had once been a professional boxer! Now I was interested. Jimmy had come through, and I had spurned his visit. The medium was right. Suddenly, I wanted to learn where Denny was and more about psychic ability.

9

I started attending the spiritualist church every Wednesday. They had what was called an open circle. I sat with about twenty people and a delightful medium called Sara. We all practised expanding our psychic abilities. I felt shy about taking part for the first couple of weeks, but I did hear voices and received names for people in the circle. I was so accurate that several burst into tears. I was still confused about where the information was coming from, but it was always startlingly correct.

I developed quickly and was invited to Southport to train with some top mediums. About six of us met every Thursday in the cellar of a home owned by medium Iris Dawson. This exclusive group of mediums had been carefully chosen and invited to the developmental circle. Iris set up video and still cameras around the room, trying to capture spirit visitors during our sessions. She was our main teacher, and I was eager to learn as much as possible from her.

One day, as I was trying to listen to Iris, a young lad appeared before me. Instantly, I recognized him as Keith Bennett, one of the most famous murder victims in British history. He was one of four children murdered by serial killers Ian Brady and Myra Hindley in the early 1960s. Keith was twelve and had been on his way to his grandmother's house when he was abducted. The couple sexually assaulted their victims before killing them and burying their bodies on Saddleworth Moor, near Manchester.

A school picture of Keith's innocent face with a toothy smile and wire-rimmed spectacles had been widely published in newspapers and shown on television. I had no doubt it was his spirit I was seeing. Keith's body was the only one never found.

'The cameras are in the wrong position,' Keith said matter-of-factly. 'They're not high enough to capture spirit.'

I tried to ignore him and concentrate on Iris. She was, after all, the expert here. How could I, a mere fledgling psychic, be seeing the spirit of one of the most recognized murder victims in England? I was sure Iris would never believe me. It would seem as if I was faking to steal attention from her. After all, I needed her to teach *me*. So I remained silent while Keith remained present to me.

'She's teaching you wrong,' he said, pointing at Iris. Even though Keith had been brutally murdered, he was a cheerful lad and exuded warmth. 'My body will never, ever be found,' he said.

I read his auric field and sensed that Keith had accepted what had happened to him and moved on in the spirit world.

When I returned home that evening, I sat and wondered why he had visited me. After that, Keith popped into my flat from time to time and carried on talking to me. I asked him lots of questions and jotted down the answers. The information he gave me was absolutely fascinating.

After Myra Hindley was sent to prison, she spent years trying to obtain her release by saying that Ian Brady had been the sole killer. But Keith told me she had definitely participated in the murders and that she had been the one who enticed him into the car with sweets.

'She tried to model herself on Marilyn Monroe,' Keith said. 'They were planning more murders. They enjoyed it. They got a thrill out of listening to the news stories about the missing children on the radio.'

I asked him what the other victims were doing on the other side, and he said they stayed together in the spirit world with various family members. Keith was waiting for his own devastated mother to arrive.

'My murderers are horrific people, and it still makes me sad that I left Mum in pain,' Keith said. 'My spirit teachers take me to visit her.'

'Will you come face to face with your killers in the spirit world?' I asked.

'It's an individual choice, but I don't want to. We are in a separate area from the killers. It is worse for murderers in the spirit world. The punishment is harsher here than on your side.'

I had heard that children who die mature to about the age of thirty on the other side, so I asked Keith why he appeared to me as a child.

'We can revert to whatever body form you will recognize.'

Finally, I got around to asking him what, for me, was the burning question: why did he come to *me*?

'Because I help other kids in similar situations when they cross over. You will get more involved with cases like this in the future, and I wanted to help you understand.'

Keith was a wonderful soul with lovely energy. He was always happy and positive, and I felt honoured to have him in my presence.

Myra Hindley spent thirty-six years in prison before dying of pneumonia in November 2002.

About six weeks after I joined Iris's group, she recognized my abilities and asked if I wanted to participate in a psychic demonstration at a small community centre near by. I agreed but, when we showed up, I saw that there were about sixty people there. My nerves flared, as I was not used to speaking in public, let alone demonstrating my psychic abilities before a large audience. I knew that I just looked like a scrawny, anxious bloke up there on that stage.

Fortunately, my anxiety didn't seem to affect my psychic abilities, because I still heard messages in all their detail. 'I have a man named Daniel here, and he's with Robert in the spirit world.' A woman gasped loudly. Throughout the session, members of the audience nodded and shouted, 'Yes!' as I spilled out facts and statements fed to me from the other side.

At the end, a man in the audience stood up and announced that he was a medium. 'Joe is the best example of mediumship I have seen in years,' he said.

I was buoyed up by the audience response that night and felt a strong sense of belonging. Perhaps I had finally found that elusive reason for my existence.

In the car on the way home, Iris seemed irritated. 'You are not ready to do readings like this,' she said. Her cruel comment was like a slap across my face. She had observed my abilities in her own circle and knew my capabilities – and she was the one who had selected me for the demonstration. I was feeling annoyed when Iris dropped me at my car.

I sped away and, almost immediately, a gorgeous young woman began to take form before me. Her energy grew until she was sitting next to me in the car, her beautiful, slender body appearing totally real. She did cheer me up. Her long, wavy hair framed high cheekbones and luminous blue eyes. Her make-up was immaculate, and she had a complexion like that of a china doll. Her clothes looked chic and expensive. I thought that if I had some-one like her waiting for me in the spirit world, it would certainly seem like heaven.

'My name is Alexis, and I lived in America,' she said. Then she told me she had died in a car accident at the age of thirty-four and was furious about it.

I pulled the car over to the side of the road so I could give her my full attention.

'That woman is not your teacher,' Alexis said angrily. 'We are your teachers!'

I realized that Alexis was a spiritual educator, like those I had seen on my jaunt to the other side with the Dengs. She told me she was helping develop my mediumship abilities so that I, in turn, could help people.

'Enough is enough,' Alexis stated firmly. 'You must not listen to Iris. You felt good about what you did tonight. Now you must trust what you are feeling inside.'

I was thrilled, and very intrigued by the lovely Alexis. Why couldn't she be alive? I realized she was telling me the same thing that Keith had told me. The teachers in spirit were a much higher energy force than anyone on earth. I decided to start going to a different class to train and learn.

I found out about another psychic training class in Blackpool and was on my way to one of the meetings one evening. Suddenly, I heard a voice. 'Drive to Maria's!' it commanded. I did not know why, but I drove to my sister's house and, as I was pulling up, a young girl came screaming into the street.

'Mum's in the fire!'

My heart lurched to attention. The previous week I had had a flash vision of a fire and smelled smoke. I had caught a scent of the same acrid smoke while in the Blackpool circle. I also remembered that the gypsy fortune-teller had warned me about a fire.

I looked to the right and saw a house which had flames shooting from the top floor. I heard a voice shout, 'Fast!'

I left the screaming girl and ran to the back entrance of the house. The door was locked but I spotted a hole where the glass was broken. I poked my hand inside, unlocked the door and stepped into a neglected kitchen. The place was already flooded with smoke.

'Anyone in here?' I shouted, but there was no response. I hurried up the stairs and threw open a bedroom door. No one was inside, so I moved to the next door and heard the spirit voice again, saying, 'She's there.'

I tried to open the door, but it was locked. Smoke billowed out from under the door, and I knew that this had to be the source of the blaze. Just like you see in the movies, I kicked at the door and, after three attempts, the lock gave way, but the door was barricaded with a heavy wardrobe and bed. The heat was so intense, it stole my breath away and stung my eyes. The thick smoke made me cough, but I shoved the furniture aside and found a woman crouched on the floor.

My first instinct was to grab her, but she didn't want to leave. I felt dizzy from smoke inhalation, but I grabbed her anyway and dragged her out of the room. I don't know now how I got her out of that burning house. Afterwards, I lay on the lawn, gasping for air as the fire brigade arrived. It turned out that the woman's name was Carol, and she had been trying to commit suicide.

The fire chief praised me for saving her life, saying that he hadn't seen anything like it in twenty years. They gave me a bravery award, along with a monetary gift, and took some photographs of me. They wanted to recommend me for a medal.

However, the police chief caught wind of it and, because of my criminal record, he put a stop to it. I didn't think it was fair, as I had turned my life around, but I do still have the award and the pictures.

Years later, I did a psychic reading for a woman who told me she was Carol's mother. She said that her daughter had been in a confused state and that her life had been spiralling downwards when she started the fire and tried to kill herself. Now she was doing fine. When I did this reading, I realized that Carol's grandfather and several of her other relatives had come to me that day and, along with my own spirit guides, had helped me save her.

With the Blackpool group, I continued to develop the new path in my life. I was very happy finally to be learning about the visions and voices which I had long considered a curse. Now, I welcomed the knowledge, and enjoyed honing my talent so that I could use my psychic abilities in a positive way. But nothing prepared me for my next spirit visitor.

One night, while I was asleep, I heard a phone ring. It was a different ring tone from my mobile or house phones. Suddenly, a young woman with long, dark hair appeared to me.

'I am the missing woman from Southport,' she said, her brown eyes pleading. An image of her mangled body flashed before me.

'It was carnage!' I heard a man's voice say.

I recognized the woman from pictures on the news. She was Lynsey Quy, a twenty-one-year-old mother of two. She had been missing for more than a year, and her husband, Mitchell Quy, had appeared on television, including ITV's *This Morning*, saying that Lynsey, who had been a barmaid, had run off with another man. Now, Lynsey's spirit was visiting me in my dream, and I knew her husband had murdered her.

'The police need to search the fairgrounds and the railway station,' Lynsey said.

I saw quick flashes of the words 'MacDowell's' and 'Baxter', and visualized a school. Then I saw tractors and old vehicles in a yard. I also saw a caravan.

I woke up confused, but quickly jotted down the details of the dream.

Lynsey Quy obviously wanted the police to discover the real truth about her disappearance.

I had no idea what to do with the information she had given me. The next day, I drove to Southport to investigate the meagre facts from my dream. As I drove, I had several flashes of the hospital. I turned on to the road that led to the hospital. The same visions glinted again, of the words 'MacDowell's' and 'Baxter'.

I knew I was being led, and followed the clues. As I drove along, I saw more visions of Lynsey's bloody, mutilated body and heard that odd word 'carnaged' again. I passed the hospital, but felt no connection there. About a mile and a half down the same road, I heard Lynsey's voice: 'Pull over!'

As I stopped on the side of the road, my car horn started to blast for no reason. I was in a residential area, and it was getting dark. I was embarrassed that the car was making such a racket, so I leapt out and banged on the bonnet. The horn stopped.

'What in the hell am I doing here?' I wondered as

I climbed back behind the wheel. I felt foolish and annoyed, but I couldn't deny that something spiritual was directing me on. I drove around the corner and was shocked to see the school that had flashed in my dream.

I felt flustered and as uncertain as a child in infant school, just learning how to navigate these new experiences. Why couldn't Lynsey just tell me what she wanted? Why did the information have to come in bits and spurts that made no sense to me?

I was angry, tired and hungry by that point and decided to return home. I started the car and shot around a cul-de-sac. As I drove out of it, I spotted a yard full of tractors and old vehicles. To the left was a business premises with large, grey vans outside. I almost died when I saw the words 'MacDowell's Furniture' painted on the side of the vans.

I pulled over and immediately saw Lynsey's murdered body in a vision. I swung my face to the left and saw a caravan with ponies on it. I was trembling. I knew Lynsey had led me to this specific location, but still felt utterly confused. What was I supposed to do with this information? I couldn't see a body there.

I didn't know it at the time, but this was the exact location at which Lynsey had been murdered: 22 Stanford Road. Clutching the steering wheel in fright, I drove home.

The next day, I returned to the area and ended up in front of a dairy shop. I was dumbfounded when I saw the name of it – Baxter's, the word I had seen in my dream! I wasn't aware of it then, but I was right outside the house where Lynsey had lived. Once again, I returned home, totally perplexed.

That week, at the psychic circle, I recounted my encounter with Lynsey. I also shared a new vision of railway tracks and a large clock. A man in the group said, 'I know where that clock is – by some railway tracks.' The next day, he took me there.

As I stood with him by the tracks, I heard Lynsey's voice: 'I'm here! I'm here!'

'Where?' I shouted out loud. If her body was here by the railway tracks, why had she told me before that police also needed to check the fairgrounds? It was all so confusing, and I still had no idea what I was supposed to do with the information.

A woman at the circle, Frieda, worked at the police station. She called the former chief inspector, who was now retired, and told him about my dreams and visions. He suggested I take the information to the police.

The police were not my greatest fans, and it was with great trepidation that I took my scribbled notes down to Southport police station the following Saturday. I chided myself as I entered the building. 'They'll think I'm mad,' I thought. It crossed my mind that they might even think that I was the murderer, because I knew so much. At that point, Lynsey was still considered a missing person.

Twenty-two officers had been assigned to investigate the Lynsey Quy case but, that morning, there was only one – female – detective at the station. I think the spirit side must have set that up, because I felt totally ridiculous and embarrassed when she walked me into an office and pulled out a notepad.

'I am a psychic,' I sputtered. 'Lynsey Quy came to me in my sleep and gave me clues on where to look for her body.'

Surprisingly, the detective treated me with respect and wrote down the information I gave her. When I had finished giving my statement, she handed me a picture of Lynsey.

'Mr Bolster, if you get any more information, please contact us,' she said.

I was relieved to tell her everything I knew and to let the police continue the investigation.

But the very next day, Lynsey showed up again. 'Joe, they're not listening to you. You must go back.'

My heart sank. Why would they believe me on my second visit if they hadn't on my first? But, knowing Lynsey was desperate for someone on earth to listen, I wrote a letter to Bob Marsden, the chief inspector, and took it down to the police station.

'This is important,' I told the desk officer. 'I am not the kind of person to waste the inspector's time. He must take this information seriously.'

I heard nothing from Bob Marsden or any of the other detectives on the case. Five months later, Marsden was taken off the Lynsey Quy investigation and a new chief inspector was hired, Geoff Sloane.

At that time, in the late 1990s, it was one of the biggest searches that had been carried out in the UK. Even though the police had detailed information from Lynsey herself via me, her family called in the famous psychic guru Uri Geller. Geller said that he psychically saw Lynsey's body by water and hotels. That was hardly a stretch, because Southport is a resort town by the sea and full of hotels. I knew he was wrong.

It horrified me to watch the police fumbling about when I had given them meticulous information from Lynsey herself on where to find her body. However, I was still confused by the two locations I had been told to go to – the fairgrounds and the railway tracks.

The new chief inspector took a fresh look at Lynsey's case and realized that she hadn't used her credit cards or bank accounts since she had gone missing. Her husband's cocky and arrogant story that she had run off with another man just did not add up. I knew he had killed Lynsey and, finally, the police pressured him into a confession.

He said that his wife had threatened to divorce him in December 1998, so he had murdered her. His brother had helped him to chop up her body. They buried her torso in the fairgrounds, near a roller coaster, and dumped her arms and legs in bushes at the railway line. That explained the two locations. Her head and hands were never found.

I later learned that it was Lynsey's grandfather who had been the male voice who helped guide me and had used the old-fashioned term 'carnaged'. After pleading guilty to the murder, Mitchell Quy was sentenced to life in prison. His brother got seven years for helping him dispose of her body.

The police never admitted that I had given them this

information long before they had even figured out that Lynsey Quy was dead.

Lynsey returned in a dream and thanked me for helping her. Even though I did not get any formal recognition for the information I supplied to the police, nor did I really want any, the experience put me on to using my abilities to help with police cases in the future.

It wasn't long before I had visions of another murder victim. One day I was sitting in my flat, and the cloudy, grey mist began to form. By now I had come to realize that this indicated that one of my spirit teachers was about to pay me a visit.

Sure enough, Alexandra Pistonie turned up, with another teacher, called John. Alexandra explained that she had assisted orphans in her former life as a nun on earth in the late eighteenth century. She works closely on the spirit side with John, who was an Orthodox priest, and they joined together to teach me how to solve murder mysteries.

On this day, the two of them showed up with a young girl. I recognized her from news reports as Sarah Payne, the eight-year-old who was abducted and murdered in Kingston Gorse on the south coast. I had seen the case on the news, but hadn't paid much attention. I certainly hadn't tried to contact her spirit. Alexandra and John brought her to me.

On 1 July 2000, Sarah had been visiting her grandparents and was playing with her two brothers and little sister in a cornfield. She decided to walk back to her grandparents' house, and her brothers later told police that she had squeezed through a gap in the hedge. Her siblings were not far behind but, when they reached the road, Sarah was gone.

They saw a white van driving towards them, with the wheels spinning as if to accelerate away. Inside, a grubby man flashed them an eerie smile, revealing crooked, yellowed teeth. They did not know at the time that Sarah was inside that van.

Sixteen days later, police found Sarah's body partially buried on the side of a road in Pulborough, Sussex. They quickly zeroed in on Roy Whiting, a paedophile notorious locally, who owned a white van. At the time of Sarah's visit to me, the police investigation had come to a standstill, as there was no other evidence against Whiting.

That day in my flat, Sarah's spirit was standing there calmly, without any bad feelings or negative energy.

'Joe, we need you to help the police solve Sarah's murder,' Alexandra told me. 'Will you help?'

The hair stood up on my arms as I realized what a privilege this was. Helping psychically solve a murder was special and important, and I knew it was a big part of the reason I had been granted psychic abilities. I accepted immediately.

'Grab a pen and paper,' Alexandra instructed.

I settled down on my couch, ready to write. Alexandra told me she and John had greeted Sarah as she passed into spirit, that they all wanted justice to be done and that this was why they had come to me.

I realized that Alexandra and John were teaching me the skills I would need to be able to help with murder cases in the future. First of all, they had me build a profile of the perpetrator, in this case, Roy Whiting.

The information came in a series of sporadic visions. They told me that the murderer worked with cars in some way, maybe as a mechanic, and that he was separated from a wife or girlfriend. This information seemed trivial, but I wrote it down, because Alexandra told me that the police would need to hear details in order to believe that I was legitimate. It was also the first step in building a profile.

Next, the spirit teachers helped me to locate the scene of the murder, as in the Lynsey Quy case. I found this part both challenging and frustrating. Why couldn't they just tell me who, what, where, when and how? But, this time, and on subsequent occasions, the information came in visual spurts. Often, I would see a location through a victim's eyes. If they were lying in a ditch, I would see cars driving by, a certain shop or another landmark.

A vision of the white van flickered before me. All of a sudden, I heard, 'Tell the police the towel is important!' I saw what looked like a cloth, and I knew it was in the van. This information was not yet public knowledge.

As I wrote down and understood the possible significance of the piece of cloth, I heard the spirit world rejoicing, as if a boisterous party was going on. The spirits were thrilled to impart this knowledge and have me understand. I had no idea how vital this clue was to be.

A few months before Christmas that year, I sent this

information by recorded delivery to the Serious Crime Squad at Scotland Yard. I wanted a signature as proof that they had received it. I never heard from them but, a couple of weeks later, new evidence was mentioned on the television news. A cloth or piece of material found in Whiting's van had been traced and linked to Sarah's killing. Roy Whiting was convicted and sentenced to life in prison. I was satisfied that I had carried out my part. I didn't need any recognition from the police.

I was still learning how to help solve murders.

10

I was still joining other psychics at Liverpool spiritualist church for readings before an audience. One evening, a group in Merseyside, Support After Murder and Manslaughter (SAMM), was holding a clairvoyants' night to raise money for their charity, and I was invited along. I was still a new medium at that point, trying to hone my abilities. The first spirit visitor that evening came for a woman in the audience named Marie McCourt.

'I have a young woman coming through saying you have connections with legal issues in London concerning your daughter in the spirit world,' I relayed.

Marie acknowledged the information to be correct.

'Your daughter passed young,' I said, repeating what the young woman in the spirit world was telling me. I then talked about various family members who were with Marie's daughter. 'Who is John?' I asked.

It turned out that John was Marie's living husband and was involved with the important paperwork Marie was handling in London. The reading I gave was rather short, and I ended it by telling Marie her daughter was fine on the other side.

After the show, Marie came up to me and told me that she ran the SAMM group and that her daughter Helen had been murdered when she was twenty-two. She had gone to London to plead that Helen's murderer should not be released from prison. I must admit, Helen's case didn't ring any bells with me; I hadn't realized what big news it was when she was killed back in 1988.

One blustery day in February of that year, Marie had planned to meet Helen for lunch and shopping in Liverpool, where Helen worked. Afterwards, they were going to drive home to Billinge, a small village near St Helens, on Merseyside. The weather was ferocious that day, with winds kicking to fierce levels. Marie cancelled the date, and the nightmare began.

Helen called Marie later that afternoon, asking her mother to prepare tea early, because she had a date that evening. Helen never showed up. Marie thought she was stuck in Liverpool because of the weather. But, as the evening wore on, with no word from Helen, Marie started to fear the worst.

Within forty-eight hours, police had arrested Ian Simms, the landlord of a pub in Billinge called the George and Dragon. The pub was just a few yards from Helen's home. Her earring was discovered in the boot of Simms' mud-caked car. Simms was the first person in British history to be tried and convicted of a murder in a case in which the body has never been found. The fact that the body was undiscovered haunted Marie for many years. She longed to give Helen a proper Christian burial. This was all public knowledge at the time of my reading but, as I say, I didn't know anything about it.

The very night of my reading for Marie, Helen came to me in a dream.

'Joe, I need you to help find my body,' she said.

Suddenly, I was astral travelling and saw a flash of Marie. I ended up in a bathroom, hovering over an old white enamel bathtub. I was confused. The bathroom was extremely narrow and looked somehow clinical. There wasn't even space for a toilet. As I floated over the tub, I heard a voice. 'The police need to go over the statements.' I knew that it was Helen speaking. 'They need to question the original suspect in order to find my body.'

Then Helen handed me a piece of clay soil and some berries picked from a wild bush. 'Visit the pub where I went missing.'

I was bewildered. I woke up and immediately wrote down the information. I was still at the point in my evolution as a psychic where this kind of information frightened me, and I was unsure how to proceed.

The next day, I called a woman I knew who attended Marie's church and asked her to set up a meeting with Marie. Helen's mother came to my flat with her sister. I told them that the police needed to re-interview their first suspect.

'Actually, there were three original suspects,' Marie said. 'Ian Simms, another lad, who was Helen's old boyfriend, and a third man, who was stalking Helen.' More confusion. I told Marie about the soil, even though it made no sense to me. She immediately knew why it was significant.

'The police could never match the dirt they found on Simms' car, on the tyres and in the boot of the vehicle. That information was on the news years ago.'

To me, however, these facts were new and, if Helen had shared them with me, the clay soil and the berries had to have some relevance now.

I asked Marie and her sister if they wanted me to contact Helen. They said yes, and she came through and flashed me an image of a group of flats above a shop.

'The date is 9 February,' Helen said. I didn't learn until much later that that was Helen's birthday, and the day she was murdered. Helen also said that Warrington Road was significant.

Marie and her sister were polite, but seemed sceptical. This didn't bother me too much; I was used to this reaction to my work, and I was exhilarated by this new information and decided to follow it up myself.

I gathered more information from Helen and tracked down additional leads. I learned that Helen's ex-boyfriend had a girlfriend who had lived at 25a Warrington Road at the time of the murder! I drove to Helen's home in Billinge to visit the George and Dragon pub. Her killer had run the place and this is where Helen had last been seen.

I sat in my car outside the pub and asked Helen for more information. Images started to flow. Helen showed me the route her body had been taken on the night of her murder. She was hauled to a church in an area called Eccleston, a village about four miles from Billinge. I visualized several landmarks along the route.

I noted the new information and entered the George and Dragon. Inside, I told the current landlord that I was psychic and asked if I could take a look upstairs, where

Helen had last been seen. It was a bit creepy climbing the steps. At the top, I was shocked to find the narrow bathroom I had seen on my astral travel – but the white enamel bathtub was missing.

The landlord explained that the police had taken the tub because it was caked with earth and clay and they had considered it evidence against Ian Simms.

I felt a surge of elation that what I had seen in my vision was matching up to reality. Was Helen telling me that the clay she had handed me in the dream was the same as the mud and earth found in the bath?

I closed my eyes there in the bathroom and clearly saw the image of the church in Eccleston and a graveyard. I also visualized the church clock. The hands were broken, and the time was stuck at twelve o'clock.

'Josh,' Helen said, but that made no sense. She also flashed an image of a silver car with no wheels.

I thanked the landlord and hurried to my car to call Marie on my mobile. 'Who is Josh?' I asked. Marie told me that Ian Simms had a cousin called Josh.

I revved up the car and drove towards Eccleston. When I arrived there, I stopped at a small grocery shop to ask for directions to the church.

'Do you know anyone in the village named Josh?' I asked the man in the shop.

'Oh, yes, a Josh lives just across the street.'

I was amazed. The puzzle was starting to piece itself together with the information Helen fed me. But what did this Josh have to do with Helen's murder? I hurried back to my car and pulled away from the shop. My mouth dropped open when I saw a silver car with no wheels parked outside what I had been told was Josh's house.

'There is DNA evidence in the attic of that home,' Helen then told me.

That had to mean that Ian Simms had been in that house the night of the murder and had left behind genetic material from Helen's body. Chills ran through me. I was excited and amazed at how powerful Helen's clues were, and by the fact that I was communicating with her spirit.

Shaking, I drove to the church and, when I found it about a quarter of a mile away from Josh's house, it matched the church in my vision. I walked through the churchyard and found a clock tower. I felt Helen's presence, and saw that the clock hands were indeed broken and fixed on twelve o'clock. I could not believe my eyes.

I felt some force pull me and, without consciously deciding to do so, I found myself walking towards the graveyard. It drew me through and right to the back, where the older headstones were located. This area was overgrown with wild plants and nettles. I stopped and closed my eyes.

What seemed like a movie spooled out in my mind. I saw Helen being dragged through the overgrown graveyard and I didn't see, but felt, her being dropped. This scared me. I remembered the berries that Helen had put in my hands along with the soil. The same berries formed part of the undergrowth here. I ran to my car and sped home, where I wrote down the information in a notepad.

Life went on as usual and, as the weeks turned into months, Helen continued to visit, offering me the same kind of information. I still did not know what to do with it. I hadn't found any evidence of her remains that day in the cemetery.

A few months later, SAMM asked me back to its clair-voyant night and, once again, Marie was in the audience. I avoided her, not wanting to offer a reading out of respect for her and Helen.

That very night, Helen came to me in a dream. 'The spit and the fire! The spit and the fire!' she shouted. I woke up and heard the words Carr Lane. I quickly wrote it down. The next morning, I pulled out a map to look up Carr Lane. To my irritation, there were a number of Carr Lanes listed in the index.

Confused, I asked Helen to explain. 'The Carr Lane in Merseyside?'

'The first suspect to be questioned,' Helen said.

'What is spit and fire?' Instantly, I saw coloured flashes and heard bangs, then I saw the words 'Warrington Road'. Next, Helen flashed me the words 'North-west Water'. After that, I saw a stream, followed by a vision of a supermarket shopping trolley.

'Carr Lane,' Helen repeated.

I felt utterly frustrated at that moment. The infor-mation meant nothing to me. Why did it have to be so complicated? I gave up trying to figure it out and ignored this new information for several weeks.

One day, I felt drawn back to my notes about Helen. I remembered Marie saying that Helen's ex-boyfriend had been one of the original suspects. I thought about the clues and the fact that this boyfriend had a new girlfriend who lived at 25a Warrington Road. I studied the notes once again and immediately realized that Helen was pointing me towards this ex-boyfriend. I also remembered that she had mentioned Carr Lane.

I grabbed the map and scanned the pages for Carr Lanes in Merseyside. I was astounded when I found one near Warrington Road. Now more motivated, I hopped back in my car and headed to the George and Dragon pub again. I wanted to retrace the path Helen said had been taken on the night of her murder.

From the pub, I proceeded to the church in Eccleston, and then followed the directions on the map into Prescott. On my approach into the village, I turned on to Warrington Road. I pulled my car over to get my bearings and was staggered to see that I was parked outside a shop that sold fireworks for parties and weddings. I straight away thought of spit and fire, the big explosions of colour and the bangs. It was so frustrating working with these hints of clues. Why hadn't Helen just told me that spit and fire meant fireworks? I was beginning to realize that communication with spirit was not always straightforward.

I looked up at the flats above the shop. One of them was 25a! I knew I was finally in the right location. I checked the map again and saw that Carr Lane was within walking distance. Everything was falling into place at last.

I drove to Carr Lane and decided to get out of my car and walk about. I took a notebook with me. Walking along the road, I saw a sign that read 'North-west Water'. Then I came upon an old supermarket trolley dumped in the middle of a stream. These were the exact images that Helen had given me.

I heard Helen's voice again: 'Here! Here! Here! Where I am, trust, trust the Holy Grail!'

What on earth did that mean? Was she speaking in metaphors? I had heard the word 'grail' in lots of different contexts. In most legends of the Grail, the hero has to prove himself worthy of it. In early tales, when the perceiver first encounters the Grail, his immaturity prevents him from fulfilling his destiny. He must grow spiritually and mentally before he can locate it again.

I certainly didn't feel like a hero at that moment. I felt thoroughly frustrated. Was Helen telling me to trust her information? And what was the significance of this location? I drove home and called Marie and her husband John and asked them to meet with me.

A couple of days later, the three of us drove back to that same spot on Carr Lane. When we arrived, I told Marie and John that I felt Helen was trying to tell me where she was. I was feeling very stressed because the McCourts looked dubious. The meeting that day came to nothing. I did, however, meet up with Marie several more times, and Helen came through and brought up the name Josh again.

By that point, I had put a lot of time and effort into the search. Now it seemed that, whichever way I turned, I was coming up against a blank wall. I was also feeling frustrated that there was no one who could back me up on the information I had received or follow up on it.

*

Years had passed since local newspapers and radio stations had reported my findings in the Helen McCourt case. And then one night, when I was in a local pub with friends, a man handed me an envelope.

'Can you look over the contents and help?' he said. 'I'll be in touch.'

It was a strange thing to happen. Apparently the man had been asking for me. I opened the envelope and scanned an A4 piece of paper with questions about the whereabouts of Helen's body outlined on a meticulously drawn diagram. I was amazed to realize that the questions had come from the police. Were they testing me? Maybe they had heard about my using my psychic ability on a previous case.

Peter Currie was the detective chief inspector assigned to the case. He was intrigued by my information about Helen McCourt and arranged a meeting with me. In order to test my psychic ability, he had me do a reading for a colleague of his and then, to document his faith in me, he had her sign a statement declaring that my reading for her was spot on.

I spent an hour with Currie and two of his colleagues. They were excited by the fact that many of the details I gave them matched the information they had gathered. I also surprised Currie by accurately naming the street where he lived and providing precise family information. Because of my visions, Carr Lane became a new focus of interest in the investigation. I was fascinated to find out how real detectives operated.

In the end, however, it all came to nothing. Helen's

body is still missing. The police have never undertaken a search at the locations I indicated. I cannot understand why they haven't tested the soil at the church graveyard and by the stream on Carr Lane. I don't know if too many years have passed, if it's a money issue or if the police don't want to admit that a psychic helped them. It frustrates me to this day.

Ian Simms still denies killing Helen McCourt, despite the fact that her earring was found in the boot of his car, and the same soil from his tyres and the car boot was in the bathtub at the pub. The police think he may have washed there after his crime. But where did that soil originate? It would only take a soil analysis to compare it with the soil in the locations Helen provided through me.

I am still in contact with Marie, who continues to mourn her daughter. In 2007, she gave me a strange portrait that Ian Simms had painted in oils in prison. It was a copy of Toulouse-Lautrec's *Jane Avril*. The French artist painted the dancer and prostitute, and Ian had copied the portrait but substituted the face of his victim, Helen McCourt. It gave me the creeps.

I held the painting in the hope of gleaning information from it through a psychic process called psychometry. This involves holding personal items such as jewellery or clothing and attempting to obtain information through them. As I held the picture, I visualized Ian Simms dipping his brush into the paints and creating strokes of colour on the canvas. He spent time, painting in detail. I saw him laughing.

I have the ability to enter a person's mind psychically through psychometry, and Simms offered a burst of visions. First, there was an abundance of yellow flowers, and then the scene changed and I clearly saw the graveyard at the church in Eccleston. Once again, yellow wild flowers flashed before me.

In the vision, as in my real visit to the graveyard, I was drawn to the older part, with its rusty fencing, blackberries, brambles and nettles. Suddenly, the old clock face stuck at twelve o'clock beamed into my mind. The image cleared.

'Josh!' a voice shouted. In my vision people were drinking ... there was something about celebrating a rugby game. I saw a fight break out, and Helen was in the middle of the chaos. Had that been what was going on at the pub on the day of the killing? The police would certainly be able to follow up on that.

I also saw a wheelbarrow in my vision and sensed that Simms had used this to transport Helen. There was a metal skip or some other huge metal object in the graveyard. Then I saw Helen's body being dragged along. There was a large space or hole in the ground, then the metal railings around the graveyard reappeared and I saw the murderer's arm dragging Helen's body. I sensed something being lifted, and Helen was thrown down some sort of hole – maybe a well. It seemed that Helen's body had to be in that graveyard, but the scene then changed to Carr Lane. I felt clothes being stripped off in this area and saw bin bags.

My final conclusion after psychically reading the

painting is that Simms was sexually attracted to Helen McCourt and is still obsessed with her.

I would love the police to follow up on my information. Marie has now been waiting two decades to find out the whereabouts of her daughter's remains. She would be grateful for closure, and I, too, would welcome some answers.

The Helen McCourt case was a good training ground for me. I told Marie McCourt that Ian Simms would eventually tell her where Helen's body is. Several times, I saw visions of Helen's funeral and I am convinced that, one day, she will be found.

11

After I had stopped working on the Helen McCourt case, I continued to attend psychic demonstrations at churches in different areas. Sometimes I would sit in the audience and study the other psychics. Some were awful, and I could psychically see that they were not connecting with anyone on the other side.

They offered up messages, and I realized that most of the audience members did not want to embarrass the psychic on stage and would kindly agree with information that was inaccurate or even incorrect. This tended to happen quite a lot in the spiritual churches, where people were eager to reach spirit and often gullible. I could understand why people were sceptical.

Later, I realized that most mediums do not train properly and have not developed their psychic talents – those who even have any in the first place. I knew I had innate abilities and had been guided into mediumship – I had been in training my entire life – but I was still at the crucial learning stage. I continued to seek out teachers and chances to practise and grow.

People often asked me if I did private readings, but I always said no. Finally, however, I decided to test the water.

My very first customers were three young women from

Skelmersdale, who invited me to a house to do their readings. I took along a new deck of Tarot cards. I really had no idea how to read them, but I perused the instructions before I arrived and memorized one of the card spreads. I felt I needed to look professional and, every time I had been to a psychic, they read Tarot cards.

I was nervous sitting in a back bedroom with the first girl who wanted a reading. I shuffled the cards, trying to look as if I knew what I was doing, and laid nine on the table in the shape of a cross, just as the instructions said I should. I thought the cards would structure the reading, but their meanings were all muddled up in my mind. I had no idea how to read them and flushed, wondering what to say.

Immediately, my clairaudience, or gift of hearing, kicked in, and I heard that the young woman was taking a two-year college course.

'You just got out of a relationship, and that's why you are here to see me,' I repeated from the voice message. I tossed a few more cards on the table, but the information came from the voice, not the cards. I felt like a sham using the cards for protection; the readings went well as long as I listened to the voice.

'Do you know Linda? She's just had a baby,' I said. 'Your mum and dad separated when you were four.'

The women were impressed by the accuracy of my readings, which built up my confidence. Then someone knocked on the door, and one of the girls' parents came in, along with a wave of negative energy.

There I was, sitting with my bogus Tarot cards, and

the father wanted a private reading. My heart sank. I immediately knew he was a sceptic, and his low energy permeated the entire room. The women left so that I could do the reading.

'Do you want a Tarot card reading, or a psychic reading from my mind?' I asked.

'You tell me.' He shrugged his shoulders. He was big, with bulging muscles, and I was engaging in what he considered to be hocus pocus in his house.

My face burned red. The man's voice was intimidating, but I decided to match his bravado, a trick I had learned on the streets as a kid. 'Do you want the cards or what I hear?'

'You tell me.'

'I'll tell you what, mate. I'll do you a spirit reading rather than the Tarot cards.' I closed my eyes and prayed to Mary, Mother of God, to feed me information and get me out of this mess before the brute kicked my head in.

Instantly, I heard a name. 'I'm getting the name Jimmy.'

The big guy didn't acknowledge what I had said.

The information flooded into my brain. 'I see Jimmy in hospital. Something to do with a cigarette lighter. I heard somebody shout, "John". Now I can see something to do with Walton Prison.'

'Fucking stop!' the man begged. 'Fucking stop the reading!' He changed his attitude immediately, and told me that Jimmy had been a friend and had recently died of cancer in hospital. He pulled a lighter out of his pocket.

'Jimmy gave this to me,' he said, and bowed his head

for a moment. 'John was Jimmy's mate, and I just got out of Walton Prison. That was amazing. When can I have another reading?'

'Come to see me again in six months,' I said, inventing the time frame to make things seem authentic. I wanted to whoop with delight. I felt as if I had won the lottery.

'I wasn't sure about this stuff,' the man said. 'I sat with Jimmy in hospital when he was dying. I wanted to know if there really is an afterlife. I was just giving it a go with you.'

I did a reading for his wife, too, and relayed the information that her dad had died of heart and chest conditions and was in the spirit world. 'Your dad was cremated. I see a box of ashes. Did your dad fall in the River Mersey?' I asked. 'Spirit is showing me flashes of ashes, then your dad going into the Mersey.'

'We had my dad cremated, then scattered his ashes in the river,' the woman said, with tears in her eyes.

I left that house excited that I could now go and do private readings. Little did I know then that I had plenty more to learn and that not all my readings would go so smoothly.

Shortly after that first attempt at a private reading, word got around Liverpool and people started booking me. I always went to their homes and often gave several readings on one booking. People in Liverpool give mediums a tough time – they want a truly gifted reader. One time, I was called to Huyton, a suburb of Liverpool, where six people had hired me for readings.

A mannish-looking woman greeted me at the door. 'You'd better be good, or we'll kick you out and not pay you.'

'I have a gun in my boot as well,' I quipped, pulling her back down to earth.

I told the first woman that her mum had died within the past four months of a brain tumour and was with her sister Ann in the spirit world. I was beginning not only to hear the information but had realized that, if I stared at the person then quickly shifted my eyes to the side of them, I could actually see a spirit show up. It was often as if I were conversing with a full-bodied human but, at other times, I had only a pale image or outline of the spirit, enough to know if it was male or female.

This particular group was very impressed with how accurate I was, but that wasn't always the case. I wasn't satisfied with myself because the quality of my readings varied. Some flowed easily but, with others, very little information came to me. Sometimes, no spirits would show up to feed me information and I'd realize that the person I was reading – and this was especially the case with young people – did not have anyone contactable in the spirit world.

In cases such as these, I began to read auric fields. I knew that everyone is surrounded by an auric, or energy field, because I could see it. I didn't understand this at the time, but the aura contains all of our history, and I found I could tap into it. Feelings, thoughts, emotions and past happenings were relayed back to me as if someone were speaking them. I experimented with reading auric fields, trying to understand my abilities, which had tormented me for so long.

On one occasion, a pleasant group of women invited me to a house and, when I was reading the first woman, her father came through and said he was with her nephew on the other side. It was a powerful reading for her and, as usual, I tape-recorded it, so that she could listen to it again.

I was conducting the readings in the living room and, after I had read three of the women, I heard them in the basement playing back their tapes.

'He's just brilliant!' one of them gushed, but I wasn't seeking accolades. With each reading, I gained confidence that the information bestowed upon me was accurate. Now, rather than kudos, I was more concerned with figuring out how the process worked.

The fourth woman entered the living room for her reading. Her mother instantly appeared in solid form. 'Tell my daughter I'm here.'

'I already have your mother here,' I told the woman. 'She was fifty-six when she died.'

'Yes.'

'Her name is Margaret.'

'Yes.'

'She's standing right here.' I pointed to the space next to me.

The girl went berserk. 'She is not!' she shouted.

I went over the information again, and she agreed with

157

everything I said but, when I pointed to where her mother was standing, she snarled again. 'No! She's standing over there.' She pointed to the corner.

I was confused, because I could see her mother; I knew I was right.

Suddenly, the grandmother of this girl appeared in spirit. 'She thinks she is clairvoyant and is pretending she sees her mother,' the grandmother told me.

I asked the girl, 'Do you want me to proceed with the reading?'

She didn't answer.

'Stop the reading,' her mother said. 'She's been drinking and is not mentally well.'

I had pretty much seen it all in my life, so I understood what she was saying.

Another time, eight women asked me to do readings for them at a house in Moss Side, a rough area of Manchester riddled with crime and gun violence. Everyone at the house was black. You rarely saw a black person in my part of Liverpool, and I was a bit nervous, worried about how to behave.

The first two readings went fine. The women were great, and I relaxed. But, before the third person entered, a voice told me it would be a man and that he had no money to pay for a reading and planned to rip me off. 'Proceed with the reading anyway,' the spirit urged.

What the spirit said disturbed me but, when the man entered and took a seat, a young male immediately appeared to me and said he was this man's brother. As if it were on television, a scene unreeled before me of this brother jumping over a counter to rob a store. There was gunfire, and he was shot dead and fell to the floor. I related this to the man, and he burst into tears. 'Your brother is saying to turn your life around.'

The man looked at me with tear-filled eyes. 'Yes, my brother was killed during an attempted robbery.' He shook his head in disbelief. 'I've just begun to turn my life around. I'm working with kids, to keep them in school.'

I could tell that the information provided by his brother through me had touched him deeply.

All of a sudden, he jumped up. 'Wait here. I'll be back in fifteen minutes.'

The man ran off, and I continued reading for the women. Sure enough, fifteen minutes later, he returned with the money to pay me in full. This reading showed me why my life had sometimes been so tough before: it was all part and parcel of my becoming a medium. I had to understand the various levels of energy, from happiness to deep despair. In order to understand others' problems, I needed to have experienced problems myself.

The spirit world gave me a glimpse into this man's future. He would indeed change his life and help children with reading and their other studies.

At my next group of readings, a teenage girl sat down before me. I suddenly saw a young man named Lee on a motorbike. He'd been thrown over the handlebars and had died. He told me that the girl in front of me was his girlfriend and that she was only nineteen. The girl and Lee both cried over their reunion. The girl was shocked at the information coming through, but also felt peace, knowing he was okay.

'He says you must move forward with your life. You do not have to wait for him. You have a future and need to have children.'

Her grandfather also came through to say hello. 'This is your mum's dad,' I said.

I was learning how to organize and structure the private readings so that I could understand the spirit communication. Many of the spirit visitors had no idea how to come through, so I made some rules. I visualized my parents and trained the spirits to walk towards my mum if they were on the maternal side of the family, and towards my dad if they were on the paternal side. This worked well and enabled me instantly to understand what I was seeing.

After this particular good-quality reading, an older woman came in and asked for a reading for herself. She was the teenage girl's mother.

'I have your dad here in the spirit world,' I told her.

'Yes.'

'I'm getting the name Tom, Tommy or Thomas.'

'No.'

I gave her a date and told her that Tom said it was his birthday.

'No.'

I was becoming frustrated. 'Your dad says you were with him at his bedside when he died.'

'No.' She leaned over and muttered, 'I won't tell anyone in the house that you weren't able to read for me.'

By this point, I trusted the information that spirit supplied in private readings. 'I don't care if you tell the world and his wife. I know this information relates to you.' I was sure of it.

She stood up, opened the door and collapsed on the floor.

The teenage girl came running to her. 'Get up, Mum!'

It turned out she was drunk on vodka. I asked her daughter about Tom and the birth date, and everything I had said was correct. The readings were certainly learning experiences, but I did feel that I was evolving professionally.

Another thing that started to evolve was, however, my own drinking.

I had never been much of was a drinker before. I had enjoyed the odd pint when I was younger but, later, I preferred to drink iced or soda water, even at the pub. Alcohol just didn't interest me.

After Denny died, I went into a bit of a decline and questioned everything. I was still terrified of mediumship. The only life I knew was wheeling and dealing. But the paranormal world was taking over my life, whether I liked it or not.

Spirits came frequently to my flat. It had been bad enough when I was a child, but now they pestered me constantly, in my own space, when I was alone. Spirits that looked like fully fledged humans moved about me, along with lights and colours, mostly various hues of blue and purple.

After the Helen McCourt case, my stamina was depleted. One evening, a horrible energy entered my flat. I tried to push this dark force away from me and, in my mind, physically fought it.

The male entity came back and was around for an entire week. He told me he had murdered someone on earth. I was so freaked out by all of this that I went down to a shop around the corner called Bargain Booze.

I knew nothing about wine; I just scanned the labels, looking for the one with the highest volume of alcohol. I bought one that had 'Chardonnay' on the label which was 14 per cent. I ran home and drank two glasses. I immediately relaxed and felt a bit tipsy. I hadn't felt this great in years. My problems seemed to melt away, and the spirits disappeared. It was heavenly. I wanted to feel like this all the time.

I quickly acquired a taste for wine and, every night, after private readings or spirit circle at church, I panicked at the thought of returning home to what seemed to me like an amusement park for spirits. To gain control, I started drinking. Eventually, I was guzzling up to two bottles a night. I brushed off the idea that I was over-indulging. For the next two and a half years I continued with the private readings, then came home and got drunk.

After a while, wine no longer did the trick, so I switched to vodka or brandy, but still occasionally drank wine. I ate badly and felt awful physically.

One night, I attended a psychic demonstration, and the medium came to me in the audience and said, 'You need to get a grip on your life. You are drinking too much.'

I felt ashamed, but the medium told me to start meditating to get my head together. She suggested I meditate in the bathroom; the spirits would be less likely to pursue me there. I had never heard *that* before.

Knowing that my guides and teachers could see me drinking and ruining my life made me feel consumed with guilt. So, instead of meditating in the bathroom, I drank in there. I sat on the floor or on the toilet and downed entire bottles of wine. I felt safe in my bathroom, thinking my guides couldn't see me.

One day, Great-uncle Tom visited. 'You must stop drinking, Joe, or you will die.'

Seeing his human-like form standing in my living room shocked me to the core. Had he been peeking through the bathroom keyhole?

'You are wasting time. You need to get your life in order. You aren't developing and are stuck in your comfort zone.'

I knew Tom was right. I had the private readings down to a comfortable routine. I was giving surface readings, offering mostly names and a few easy facts. It was easier than checking the source of the information. I knew I was deliberately not connecting strongly enough with the messengers.

I thought I was coping, but Tom's visit was a real wake-up call. For the past seven months, I had not felt totally comfortable with the readings I had been giving. I knew they were poor quality because of the alcohol. I didn't want to be a medium any more.

At a church in Liverpool, I joined a healing class that

took place on Thursday nights. I met a nice guy who said he worked with an Indian spirit guide. Despite liking him and having my own spirit guides, I was still sceptical about him. He asked me several times to come to his flat for a healing, but I turned him down. Finally, I said yes and, when I got there, I was surprised to see a huge Indian guy. He told me he was not working with the guy who had asked me to come for the healing but was assisting *me*. I was shocked and didn't say anything to my friend. He had been right, in any case: I did feel better after the healing session.

Back at the healing group, I saw the Indian guide at my side. I laid my hands on a person, and the Indian moved them to where healing was needed. I eventually closed my eyes and allowed my hands to move to specific locations on the body. Then the Indian told me what was wrong.

I preferred the healing to mediumship. It had been several weeks since Great-uncle Tom had warned me about my drinking, but now I decided to go cold turkey. I felt bad for days and was constantly tempted to drink, but I knew that was the easy way out. I had a strong inner knowledge that I had to stop drinking.

I never drank another drop.

12

Several weeks after I had decided to stop drinking, I was in Bournemouth, where I noticed a rash on my arms. At first I thought it was heat-related as I had been outside most of the day in the sun, but then I started to feel unwell and had a splitting headache. My spirit helpers Tom, the priest and the nun popped in. They seemed worried.

'See a doctor,' Alexandra, the nun, said.

The doctor checked my rash and, without offering any diagnosis, told me to take a painkiller for my headache.

Back in my car, I felt so ill that I decided not to stay in Bournemouth but to make the five-hour journey back to my flat. I wanted to crash out on my own bed and recover. As I drove, I felt worse and worse. I could barely concentrate and stopped being able to focus on the road. I pulled over several times and, 130 miles into the trip, I stopped at a service station to use the toilet. I had double vision and could barely walk.

'Call an ambulance!' Tom shouted.

I got back in my car but was too sick to do anything but fall asleep right there. I woke up, drove a bit, then pulled to the side of the road where I again lost consciousness. Early the next morning, I finally arrived home. The sweat was pouring off me and I noticed that the angry rash was now covering my body. I called my sister and she rushed me to the doctor.

'How long has he had this rash?' the doctor asked. 'It looks like meningitis.' He called an ambulance and had me taken into hospital immediately.

Doctors ran some tests, including giving me a painful lumbar punch in my spinal column. I have never felt so ill in my life. Sure enough, I had viral meningitis – fortunately, not the fatal variety, but I was extremely sick in hospital for five days.

While there, Alexandra visited and said I would be okay. That was comforting, but I was ill for the next month.

During that time, a new spirit teacher arrived. This entity was different from the other teachers. He was profoundly knowledgeable.

'You will be going to school soon,' he told me. 'You need to learn more about mediumship.' He said his name was Arthur Findlay, which didn't mean anything to me then.

Around the same time, a spirit called Ruby showed up. He was flamboyant, to say the least: a male cross-dresser, Ruby was dressed up to the nines in high heels and a feather headdress.

'I work with all the best people in show business, sweetie,' Ruby said, showing off in his sequinned gown. Ruby was openly gay, and I wasn't used to being around people as way out as him. 'I'm here to soften you up, gorgeous man,' he purred. 'You're much too tough and blunt. I'm going to mould you into a more relaxed, humorous figure, big boy.'

Ruby stuck close for the next year, despite numerous efforts on my part to expunge him from my life. I have nothing against gay people, but I am not into men blowing me kisses, which Ruby did on a regular basis and found hilarious.

'See, you're softening up, gorgeous,' he cooed.

I felt that he was messing with me and tried my best to escape him, but Ruby was a perfect example of guides and teachers who enter our lives to teach specific lessons. Obviously, I needed to learn how to lighten up, and there was no way I was going to be able to avoid his flamboyant presence.

A couple of months after I had recovered from viral meningitis, a woman named Mary White called me from Workington Spiritual Church in the Lake District.

'Joseph, I am the president of the church, and a medium artist we had scheduled to appear tomorrow has cancelled,' she said. 'Are you a medium artist?'

The Workington Spiritual Church was about a hundred miles from where I lived, and I knew they only took the best mediums. But I was definitely not a psychic artist.

I heard Ruby say something in my ear. 'Tell her you can do a clairvoyant show, sweetie.'

'We're looking for someone in the mediumship field,' Mary replied. 'What are your credentials? Can you read flowers?'

Ruby was driving me crazy, telling me to tell Mary that

I did indeed read flowers. I couldn't believe I actually said it.

'Can you come tomorrow?' Mary asked.

Unbeknown to her, Ruby was blowing me kisses and shouting in my ear, 'Yes! Yes! Well done, gorgeous ... spectacular performance, bravo!'

I had done smaller shows in Liverpool with other mediums but had never performed in a big church or done a solo demonstration. Mary looked me up and down when I arrived for the show, checking how I was dressed. I must say, she intimidated me, as did the seventy or eighty people in the audience.

'You must say an opening prayer and give some sort of philosophical outline for half an hour,' Mary explained.

That filled me with alarm. I had no idea how to say a prayer, and I certainly didn't have thirty minutes of inspiring prose in my head. In no time at all, I was on stage, with my heart fluttering and my legs like jelly.

'Stand up straight and concentrate. Pull in your cute behind!' Ruby commanded. 'This is your opportunity, sweetie. Work your stage; embrace your audience with your gift. Breathe, darling. Break a leg, you gorgeous specimen.'

I didn't know if I should laugh, cry or run out of the building. I think I said the fastest prayer in church history. What could I say to these people that was life affirming?

'I'll tell you what you can bloody say to them, sweetie. Tell them not to criticize a person's sexual orientation or religion,' Ruby instructed. He burst into laughter, blowing me a kiss and offering a sensational wink.

Camp as ever, Ruby had me over a barrel. I had nothing else to say, so I repeated pretty much what he fed into my mind about the way in which we discriminate against homosexuals in our society. 'We don't even talk to them, yet we act as if we know what they are like. We do the same thing to people for their religious beliefs.'

The audience seemed to be loving it. But, after nine minutes, the words no longer came. I knew Mary had wanted me to speak for half an hour, but I had run out of inspiration. I told the audience to think about what I had said and ended my speech abruptly.

The audience looked as bewildered as I felt.

Quickly, Mary pushed a table covered with flowers in front of me.

I froze. My God! She really did want me to read flowers. They smelled like flowers you would have at a funeral. Each stem was numbered.

'Joe has to soften up and become the flower, my little rose petal,' Ruby teased. 'Pick up the sensitivity of the bloom. Become one with the flower and let the awareness flow, sweetheart.'

If Ruby hadn't already been dead, I could have killed him. But he was very much alive on the other side, and he was my only lifeline that day.

Some of the members of the audience had brought a flower from their garden, so each blossom represented a person. I had to do it. Feeling like a fool, I picked up the first stem and was shocked when it spoke to me straight away.

'The flower is saying that you can't make up your mind

which way to go on a current project,' I told the person who had brought the bloom in to be read. 'You live by the sea, and I see you connected with water.'

Every time I picked up a flower, I was actually reading the person who had brought it in. Some people burst into tears when they heard the message I passed on to them. If the flower was weighty, I linked it to heavy emotions. Ruby guided me on how to read the flowers all the way through. It was a real lesson in mediumship.

I realized I had needed Ruby's encouragement to agree to this show in the first place, and I had to admit that the flowers did indeed have power. The whole experience really bolstered my confidence.

In 2002, we were still renting a space for our spirit circles and other activities in Skelmersdale. We charged people a pound to attend. The spirit circles had started with a dozen or so people and, by this point, up to a hundred people from all over the north-west were showing up, wanting me to give them readings.

Great-uncle Tom was the real star of the circle. He turned up every Wednesday with the rest of the crowd and even showed himself a few times. Tom loved the group because we all worked on developing our skills. Alexandra and John also took part, and Ruby wanted to join in the fun too. It just went to show that everyone has a variety of spirit guides who come for different purposes. The expanded spirit circle carried on for several years.

It was in this group that I heard some other mediums talking about an amazing school called the Arthur Findlay

College. I was amazed to hear the name of my spirit teacher, who I now learned had died in 1964, before I was even born. He had been an eminent medium and was the honorary president of the Spiritualists' National Union.

When Findlay retired from his business career, he purchased the Stansted Estate in Essex, with hopes of building it into a spiritualist college. When he died, he willed the estate and an endowment to the union. The Arthur Findlay College is now the most highly respected school of its kind in the world. People flock from the four corners of the earth to attend classes there and learn from the most renowned mediums alive. I hoped to attend some classes there one day. I was impressed by what people were saying, but I didn't tell a soul that I was working with Arthur Findlay's spirit. They wouldn't have believed me.

My time at the Skelmersdale church spirit circle had taught me a lot, but now it was time to move on. I decided to take those classes at Arthur Findlay College. Although I now felt comfortable doing readings in front of ninety people, I also felt that something was lacking. Even though I received some great messages, at other times I was unfocused. I definitely had my share of guides on the spirit side but now I needed earthly teachers as well. I decided to settle in at the Stansted Estate.

The college asked me to fill out an assessment form about my psychic/medium experience. I was proud to write that I ran my own circles, with seventy to a hundred participants. I was placed in a week-long class with Paul

Jacobs and Janet Parker, who were considered the top teachers at the school.

Paul was an internationally renowned medium, and Janet proved to be equally talented. The first day of class, I felt a bit smug, having what I considered was vast experience in the psychic realm. They had me a do reading, and I was pleased with it when I had finished.

'You're not very good,' Paul said. 'You're only average.'

Talk about a body blow. Welcome to the world of Arthur Findlay College!

'Darling, you're in for the shock of your life,' Ruby said. 'Now the teaching begins, sweetie.'

Paul and Janet's class was difficult. On the second day, I gave what I thought was an excellent reading.

'That was rubbish,' Paul hissed. He really was strict and could be very irritable. 'Is that all you have to offer?' British mediumship is all about proper development, and Paul's style was to stomp on any preconceived ideas of how good you thought you were.

'A good medium must link with a character in the spirit world,' Paul said. 'Who was offering the information you gave?'

This confused me. The information always flowed easily to me but, if it didn't come from my recognized guides and teachers, I wasn't sure of the source. I had never thought about it in that way before, and was intrigued.

Paul taught us to zero in on the spirit who is supplying the information and, if you're a good medium, to find out what this person did for a living on earth and how old they were when they passed. In other words, you had to home in on the source.

'There is a huge difference between psychics and mediums,' Paul taught. 'Psychics pick up earthly feelings and thoughts and gather information from the auric field. That is easier than communicating with the spirit world, which is what is called mediumship.'

This information astounded me. All of a sudden, my natural abilities seemed inadequate. I had developed my own ways of communicating, and they included mixing psychic readings of people's auras *and* chatting with spirits. Usually, those lines blurred. I knew this made for interesting readings that enthralled an audience, but my method did not fit Paul's rigid structure.

Paul was a purist and insisted we should be getting our information from the spirit world. Most people at the college dipped into the psychic level and mixed the two. It is extremely difficult for most psychic/mediums always to distinguish between psychic or spirit input.

I was devastated and lost all my confidence. I was so worried about applying these new, stringent rules that I found I could no longer do the readings. Here I was, with the world's best teachers, who could see the spirits we connected with, and I just felt intimidated and couldn't even feel my regular guides. Had I lost my means of communication with spirit?

Even though I was scared to death, I was interested enough to keep going. Something deep inside urged me on.

One night, while I was asleep in room 207, a spirit man

visited me. I awoke with a twinge in my body from my head to my feet – that's how close he was standing to my bed. It was Arthur Findlay. My heart started to race.

'Now, the real knowledge begins,' he said. 'You are on a new pathway.'

I was too embarrassed to tell anyone that the college's founder was visiting me. I stuck with the course, paying £450 to attend classes every two months. Paul and Janet took me under their wing. Paul, especially, wanted me to grasp on to an energy in spirit and to practise gleaning specific information. He talked me through an exercise of calling in a spirit and having them sit down in a chair. 'Now ask the spirit to stand outside the location where they lived on earth,' Paul guided. 'Ask them what they are seeing out of their front door. Get specifics. What is the name of the road?' Basically, Paul was urging me to structure what the spirits were telling me.

During the long lull between classes, I practised these exercises and, when we went back, he had us demonstrate in front of the class.

First, a female student tried it.

'That was terrible,' Paul said.

I felt confident when it was my turn, but Paul criticized me as well. I felt like punching him.

'You wanted to kick my head in,' Paul said to me after class.

'Yes, I did!'

'Why don't you just do what I told you? You need to concentrate on delivering the messages.'

My self-doubt flooded back. The structure was fine,

but Paul wanted us to perform the way he did. The more I tried his lessons, the more I realized that it just didn't feel right for me. Although Paul was a fascinating teacher, I didn't want to be his clone. I needed my own style and to work the way I knew was true to my own abilities.

I decided to use what Paul and Janet had taught me about the differences between psychic and medium skills and how to stay in touch at both levels, but I thought it was important and right to mix the two. Once I'd made this decision, things really started moving on.

My own guides kicked in and showed me a new technique. I would use mediumship to connect with a spirit, as Paul and Janet had taught me. I found that this spirit didn't know what the person I was reading was thinking so, then, I would tap into the person's auric field and feed information back to spirit. It was give and take, and it worked brilliantly.

Paul and Janet's method had been accepted practice for many years, but everyone needs to follow their own individual path and guidance. Paul and Janet certainly opened up new horizons for me, and I am eternally grateful for that. That knowledge, along with my decision to mix my psychic and medium skills, allowed me to progress at an extraordinary rate.

Findlay told me I needed to widen my knowledge base so that I could help more people. I began to read up on all kinds of medical issues, such as heart disease, cancers and other common illnesses. I realized that my strongest readings involved murders, suicides and car crashes.

Findlay explained that this was because I had had real-life experience in those areas.

'The mediumship world does not understand that,' Findlay said. 'People live specific lives to learn and understand different areas of knowledge. These areas are where the mediumship is strongest for that person. This is how mediumship will evolve in the future, with experts in every line of earthly life.'

I found this fascinating. Findlay said that the earth had turned a corner and was heading towards this modern mediumship. The rigid structure of old mediumship is fantastic and important, but the future is about knowledge. I was beginning to understand, but it would still take me another two years to pull all this information together.

It was now 2004, five years since Denny had died and I followed my path into psychic mediumship. I was still at Arthur Findlay College. Paul and Janet recognized my ability and brought me into classes with them as a student teacher. I considered this an honour, as it usually takes twenty to twenty-five years to develop to this level. But I had been doing it all my life. It was a real privilege to have the world's top teachers helping me to advance. They were wonderfully supportive.

I didn't tell Paul and Janet that I was secretly teaching my own way or that the students loved it. Although I was twenty years younger than my teachers, I knew it was time for their wisdom to evolve.

As a consequence of its international reputation, it was

common at Arthur Findlay College to have a class full of students from abroad. Lots of Americans came, and they were often the most cocky, boasting that they were better than John Edward, a medium popular in the United States. I have watched Edward on his television show, studying him, and consider him one of the most gifted mediums in the world. I love his casual, laid-back style and his empathy for people. These students were in for the same rude awakening that I had battled with in the beginning.

In my classes, I kept things simple. I preferred to help students grow as individual mediums. First, I would ask them why they wanted to be a medium and to define what they thought were their greatest strengths in the field. These were the two most important questions of all. From their answers, I could always tell if they were truly talented or just showing off. Unfortunately, there was a lot of ego over substance. The power that can come with mediumship can be alluring.

Of course, I taught the students the difference between psychic readings and mediumship. Most of my students loved being psychic but hated mediumship and initially fell to pieces in the same way I had. But I also honed their specialized skills and helped them merge the two worlds together. I wanted them to be their true selves and branch into their own specialties, in the way Arthur Findlay had explained was our future.

As I became more popular among the students, other colleges in the Lake District and Oxford called and asked me to teach. I was also approached by Hafan Y Coed in

South Wales, a smaller and less glamorous school. It was more affordable than Arthur Findlay College, and I enjoyed teaching there. The students were excellent and very down to earth.

The famous British medium Tony Stockwell also taught at Hafan Y Coed. He had his own show on television, which was very popular, and his classes always filled straight away. I was very pleased when I got into one of his classes as a student. Tony demonstrated his trance-mediumship. I thought he was truly gifted.

On the first day, I met a beautiful, long-legged blonde called Claudine Hope. She was bubbly and fun, and we joined up to do readings for one another.

'Your mum passed recently,' I told her. 'She had difficulty breathing and was on oxygen. She is showing me a reindeer skin she hung on a large wall in the farmhouse where you lived. She's telling me you gave the reindeer skin a haircut and blamed your sister to avoid punishment.'

Claudine was stunned by my accuracy. I learned that she was a professional dancer and actress, and I was pleased that she recognized my talent. I really enjoyed her company that week.

One evening, after dark, Stockwell split the class into two groups and took us outside to psychically explore the college grounds. He took one group and put me in charge of the other. I was happy to be with Claudine, but the mosquitoes were biting me all over my arms and legs.

'Let's go somewhere interesting,' I said, and led the

group to a graveyard next to the college. Once there, we noticed a large hedge and heard the other group working on the other side. Feeling naughty, I hushed my group and moved them to our side of the bushes. We began making scary noises, and I called through the hedge: 'Tonnnyyyy.'

The other group began to laugh, so we walked over to the gravestones and formed a circle. 'Time to get serious,' I said.

Suddenly, a stern voice spoke to me. 'Get out of the graveyard *now*! You are being very disrespectful, and it's not visiting hours.'

I was the only one who heard this terse warning, but I relayed it to the group. The students were terrified and ready to burst into tears. I was frightened too.

It came into my mind to say a group prayer and apologize, but the voice also said that we really had to mean it. I recited a proper prayer with a sincere apology, and the voice came back: 'We accept your apology and you are quite welcome to stay.' I shared this with the group, but they still wanted to leave.

The voice had been so reassuring, however, that I talked them into staying. I gazed over the gravestones and was startled to see a young lad appear by one of the headstones. He was a good fifteen feet away, but I read him and learned that he had been nine years old when he died. I told the group, but they couldn't see him. We moved to his headstone and, sure enough, the dates declared that he had lived to the age of nine.

We formed another circle, and a man appeared. He

told me he had been twenty-nine when he passed. He said he was standing with his parents by their grave. As we approached the headstone, we saw that he was indeed buried next to his mum and dad.

That evening taught me to respect graveyards as sacred resting places. Some spirits stay connected to their graves and want respect.

13

I really think it was fate that stepped in and made me hook up with Claudine Hope. After the class with Tony Stockwell, she asked if she could arrange my first show in a theatre. Claudine was at home on stage and in show business and knew how to handle all the details. I was impressed with this lovely woman and let her book me a show at the Neptune Theatre in Liverpool.

'It's one of the smaller theatres,' Claudine said. 'It only holds about four hundred people. I thought I'd start you out small.'

I gulped a bit at the sound of an audience that size but, now that I had made numerous appearances in front of smaller audiences, my nervousness didn't last long, and I felt confident that I would be able to do the work for which I had been trained.

However, Claudine totally messed up that confidence on the night of the show. An hour and a half before the curtain was due to go up, when I was ready to breeze on stage and do my readings, she said: 'You haven't done the technical part.'

I had no idea what she meant. Then the floor crew wired me up to a microphone, performed soundchecks and perfected the lighting. Claudine explained that music would be used to create the mood and that there would be a voice-over introduction. I went from hopping straight out in front of a group of people to this massive new level of showmanship in the space of one hour. I broke into a sweat.

The microphone and fuss irritated me but I had to admit that Claudine knew her stuff. I knew mine, too, and it was time for our two areas of expertise to merge. My biggest concern was connecting with spirit under these conditions.

'You don't understand,' I pleaded with Claudine as we stood in the wings just before my entrance. 'I am used to a certain ambiance, and any disruption will affect my performance. These lights, the music –'

Claudine straightened my tie with a firm gesture, showing me that she was in charge. 'Nonsense! Do you understand the format and know how to start the programme?'

My mind was blank.

Claudine reminded me that the Neptune was a great opportunity, but I really had no idea how I would get on that evening. She took both of my hands and began a prayer. 'Let's call in your guides. You'll be great, Joe – really. Just do what you do.'

The music started and I heard the voice-over introducing me. The curtain went up, and there I stood, feeling totally naked on that big stage. My heart hammered and missed a few beats, and I was certain the audience could see how nervous I was. On the stage was a stool and a table with a jug of water on it, and I kept a hand on the table in case I collapsed.

In a strangled voice I managed to squeak out, 'Good evening, ladies and gentlemen –' I was like a shadow of myself on that stage but, thanks to my table crutch, I managed to keep it together, peering out over the vast audience. I threw out a few facts about the paranormal world and, before long, the messages began to flow.

After that, I relaxed and felt at ease. I can't say it was a great night of mediumship, but I survived. Honestly, if I had been in that audience, I would have asked for my money back. But people seemed to enjoy themselves, despite the fact that there were a lot of people who said 'No' to pieces of information I relayed to them. I felt the size of the show destroyed my rhythm and I was, on the whole, dissatisfied with my performance.

Claudine thought it was hilarious. 'I tossed you in the deep end so you would learn to swim quickly.'

Having choked on too much water in that deep end, I prayed my lungs would clear.

I worked on my skills at performing in large theatres over several years, but it was murder cases that continued to draw me. Going on the experiences I had had in my life, I began to realize they were my speciality.

One summer evening in 2003, I was attending a clairvoyant demonstration at a hotel. A woman was selling copies of *Paranormal News*. I was featured in an article in it that month, so I bought one. I began to chat with this woman. She said her name was Anna Smith, and she asked me for one of my cards. A few days later, she called me.

She told me that her husband had been arrested for murder, but she was totally certain that he had not committed the crime. 'I need your help, Joe,' she pleaded.

I met with Anna and began with a reading. Immediately, the murder victim, Ruth, showed up and stood behind me. 'Don't pay any attention to her. Her husband is my killer!'

I was surprised by this but tried to remain calm in front of Anna. I was unsure how to proceed. Even though Anna was adamant about her husband's innocence, I had the spirit of the victim right here, and I trusted Ruth.

'Anna, what if I get information that your husband is guilty?'

Anna didn't answer the question, maintaining that her husband had not killed Ruth and had been framed for her murder.

'If I close my eyes, I can enter an altered state of meditation and revisit the house where Ruth was killed to see who the murderer was,' I told Anna.

Ruth gave me a vision of the killer. 'Did your husband once have curly hair?' I asked.

'A long time ago.'

I asked Ruth's spirit how she knew what Anna's husband's hair had been like a long time ago, and she told me she had been a physiotherapist and that he was a former client. I did not tell Anna everything I was receiving but offered, 'I feel your husband has been in that house.'

Anna denied that this could be true, but I told her I was 100 per cent certain that her husband had been in the victim's home. I suggested we go to the house to see if I could get more information there, hoping to make it easier for Anna to take on board.

We drove to the house and approached the front gate. The moment I touched it, I had a vision of the killer entering the house, and then a quick series of scenes of the man raping and stabbing Ruth.

Purposely not passing this gruesome information on to Anna, I said, 'I feel that your husband went away for a couple days after the murder.' I had a distinct vision of the killer leaving Ruth's premises after the murder, then some flashes of camping gear.

'Yes, he did go to visit relatives at that time.'

We left the house and walked up the hill. 'Believe it or not, Anna, I feel your husband and the victim were in a hotel together before the murder.'

Anna finally admitted that her husband had met Ruth many years previously, when he was in the military, but it had only been once. He had completely denied being in her house.

Suddenly, I saw a sharp object like a knife, wrapped in a towel. I knew the killer's sperm was on this towel as well. The vision showed me the killer walking through a graveyard close to the house and leaving the towel and murder weapon by a headstone. Anna was excited by this information, but I knew that it implicated her husband.

The next day, Anna and I went to the graveyard and tried to find the murder weapon wrapped in the towel. But the cemetery was massive and looked pretty much the same all over. I could not pinpoint the exact grave I had seen in my vision.

'Can you get me a picture of your husband?' I asked Anna. Even though I had seen a clear vision of what the killer looked like, I wanted to make sure it was actually Anna's husband.

I returned to Arthur Findlay College, where I was still attending classes and, a few days later, received an envelope in the mail. Sure enough, the photograph of Anna's husband matched the man I had seen in my visions.

Ruth appeared and said, 'I told you.' She explained that Anna's husband had come for a massage a few days before the murder and had tried to leave without paying. An argument had ensued and, on 30 July, he had returned, and his anger escalated to her brutal rape and murder.

I had no idea what to do with this information. This was not what Anna wanted to hear. What could I possibly say to her? We had become friends.

'God damn it, sweetie, tell her her husband is guilty,' Ruby popped in to say.

I finally told Anna that I could no longer assist her on the case. As politely as I could, I said her husband had been on the premises and was lying. In fact, the police had found his footprints in the house and would go on to match his DNA to that found at the scene of the murder.

'He's not guilty!' Anna declared. 'I'll fight this!'

After police found hair and semen samples on the

carpet in Ruth's bathroom and matched the DNA to that of Anna's husband, he admitted that he had had sex with Ruth in the therapy room at her house but denied stabbing her six times.

Police say it was a lengthy, sadistic attack which appeared planned and had been carefully executed, including the removal of the murder weapon from the scene.

Anna's husband was convicted and sentenced to serve a minimum of nineteen years in prison. Anna is still fighting for his release.

Once the spirit world had started to open up murder cases for me, they began to flow constantly. At about six o'clock one evening I was in my flat when I felt the presence of Jill Dando, the co-presenter of *Crimewatch*.

On the morning of 26 April 1999, Jill was returning to her expensive home in Fulham in south-west London when she was shot in the head. A neighbour found her slumped on the doorstep and called an ambulance, but Jill died a few hours later in hospital.

A massive hunt for her killer ensued, with more than two thousand names of possible suspects pouring in from the public. Police finally zeroed in on Barry George, who lived just five hundred yards away from Jill's former home.

'They have the wrong man,' Jill's spirit told me when she came to my flat.

I was flabbergasted. Why had this famous woman come to me? I was still stunned whenever these cases came through. Every one was different, and each offered a unique learning experience. Once again, I had no idea what to do with the information I had been granted.

Jill told me that the police should be following up something that sounded like 'Clemons'. I was unsure if this was the name of a person or of a street. Jill wanted the authorities to question the person who lived next door to her house, because she said he might have seen somebody.

Jill suggested that a former boyfriend or someone she had been in a relationship with held a grudge against her. 'It was a hired contract,' she said. 'The killer sat in a café near my home before the murder.' She showed me the gun he used and said it was somewhere by the River Thames.

I sent this information to the crime squad at Scotland Yard, but never heard back from them.

In July 2001, Barry George was convicted of Jill Dando's murder. Although some aspects of his background may appear questionable, I feel he is an innocent man. In fact, many people in England do not believe George murdered Jill Dando either. Numerous newspaper articles and television documentaries have investigated his case, suggesting he may be innocent, but he remains behind bars.

I know Jill is not at rest because she visited me. I believe that her real killer is still at large.

Murder victims, not all as famous as Jill Dando, continued to besiege me with requests to find their killers.

During one private reading, a spirit man told me that his body was in the wall of a store on the street the Beatles made famous: Penny Lane.

One of the most touching visits was by a spirit man who came while I was doing a reading for his girlfriend. He was very emotional and said he had died as they were talking about getting married.

She burst into tears. 'Yes, we discussed it, but his cancer was getting so bad, he wasn't strong enough to marry.'

Now he looked perfectly healthy and asked his beloved if she still wanted to tie the knot. She smiled through her tears when I told her that John, the priest, was here now and had agreed to marry them.

It was a lovely ceremony, which only I witnessed on earth, and the woman left the reading happily married.

In 2004, another high-profile murder case came my way. I received a call requesting a reading from Mary Kelly. I always prefer to start readings from scratch, with no prior information from the client. On this occasion, I immediately sensed a young man in the room, and Mary started to cry.

'I'm getting some type of shooting or loud bang connected with his death,' I told her. 'I feel he was shot.'

The sixteen-year-old lad's spirit held up an article in the newspaper; his picture was on the front page. This flash of a newspaper appeared often in my readings from this point on and allowed me instantly to identify the victims.

'Mary, I am seeing that your son was shot, and that his

name was Liam. I can see the headline with his name.'

'Tell my mum five people were involved and one of them is a girl,' Liam said. He also shared with me some personal things that had happened before he was shot. 'The ambulance couldn't get to me for fifteen minutes, because the police had blocked the road and wouldn't let it through.'

'Actually, it was twenty minutes,' Mary said. 'I had a dream of my Liam, and he was showing me the palm of his hand.'

Liam told me he was trying to tell his mother the names of those involved in his killing. 'The name is Parle. It sounds like "palm",' Liam said.

I was used to spirit giving me confusing clues and understood why Mary did not connect her son's palm with a person named Parle.

'Parle,' Liam said. 'He chased me the week before my death. I threw a bicycle into someone's living room, and he shot me dead for it.' Liam was from Toxteth, a rough area of Liverpool, home to the riot of 1983.

The reading ended, and I handed Mary the audiotape I had made of it. Mary told one of the inspectors on the case about my reading, and he took the tape in as evidence. I recorded several readings for Mary during the investigation, and she passed these on to the police.

Many months later, two people, Anthony Campbell and Hanna Morgan, were arrested, and the police named Parle as the man who had pulled the trigger. He had not been caught.

The police say they based the arrests on their own

evidence. But the detective told Mary that I was 'damn, bloody good!'

At the time of writing, Kevin Parle is still on the run, and there is a £10,000 reward for information on his whereabouts. Anthony Campbell pleaded guilty and received a twenty-one-year sentence for Liam's murder. Hanna Morgan was given a one-year sentence for perverting the course of justice. Peter Sinclair got eight months for assisting an offender and Patrick Smeda was unanimously acquitted by Liverpool Crown Court.

While I was busy doing my own little bit to investigate past crimes, Claudine became my manager and sent me on a mini-tour playing theatres around England, getting me used to microphones and stages and hoping to put me in the public eye. She decided that the next step, to really raise my profile, was to try and get me on television.

She contacted a network called Your Destiny TV because it carried a live call-in programme which had various psychics on it. A pretty host sat with the psychic, and people from home called or texted questions.

Claudine actually hated the format, thinking that it would not show the range of my abilities but, at the time, UK television was saturated with popular paranormal/psychic shows, with people such as Derek Acorah, Tony Stockwell and Colin Fry appearing, and this was the only programme in which she could find me a slot.

I thought I wanted to try things out on a larger scale, such as on television, but spirit seemed to be holding me back. I figured I had more to learn and was willing to pay my dues – but I had no idea how high these dues would become.

Claudine set up an interview for me at Your Destiny TV and, for my audition, I had to read the producer, a woman called Chelsea. She was impressed with the reading and put me on the show the same day.

'Can you appear in an hour?' she asked.

Talk about being pushed in at the deep end – I didn't even have time to walk the gangplank! All of a sudden, they were explaining what I had to do: 'Just smile and let the host carry you,' Chelsea said. 'When you deliver a message, look into the camera.' They clipped on my microphone and stuck an earpiece in my ear. Now I was sitting in a tiny studio with a presenter, a camera in my face.

My heart jumped, knowing the show was being broadcast. I heard the director speaking in my ear: 'Twenty seconds, get ready.'

The presenter nudged me, and my face flushed beet-red as I heard, 'Four ... three ... two ... one. You're on!'

'I'm Chantel,' the presenter said smoothly. 'We have with us an amazing medium named Joe Power.'

I smiled like an idiot, not knowing where to look.

Chantel asked for callers, but the phones remained silent. Nobody wanted to try out this new, scared-looking bloke. The presenter had to keep talking until the programme went to a break.

Soon we were back on air, with Chantel still trying to fill time. She pointed to a crystal ball on the table. 'What do you see in that?' she asked.

I was hating every moment of this. Finally, a text did come through, from someone called Samantha. 'Can you pick up anyone in the spirit world for me?'

Speedily, a female spirit showed up, and I told Samantha it was her mother sharing her age and a message. After that, texts started to pour in, and the messages flowed easily. I at last felt comfortable. Texters complimented me on my readings and gushed about how accurate I was.

They kept me on the air live for eight hours! I was starving, sweating and exhausted. Although the readings were going fine, I thrived on the energy of a live audience, with its instant feedback. My only response on television was a silent text and Chantel.

Chelsea loved the show and asked me to appear full time. Claudine wanted me on television, so I signed on for nine months. It gave me an important grounding in television.

14

After my tenure at Your Destiny TV ended, I returned to Arthur Findlay College to take and teach more classes. I was amazed at the barrage of compliments I received from people who had really enjoyed watching me on the show. New students came from all over the country to take my class because they had faith in what I had done on television. Many joined me in classes in which I was a student myself. I was surprised by this positive feedback, and relieved. It made me realize that my true desire to use my unfolding abilities to help others had shone on television, and it had promoted my skills to a wider audience.

It was well known that Stansted Estate, where Arthur Findlay College was located, was haunted. Lights would flicker on and off, and I sometimes felt taps on my shoulder. Many students heard footsteps clomping down the corridor.

Early one morning, I was asleep in one of the rooms when a visitor showed up. In my dream state a woman hovered above my bed. I recognized her as Smelly Shirley, a character I remembered from my childhood. Shirley had lived in a grubby house near the shops in Skelmersdale and, when I was a child, everyone bullied her because she rarely washed and, basically, stank. The kids called her Smelly Shirley. I didn't like it when my mates teased her, shouting out that cruel nickname. Although I still wanted my mates to think I was cool, I would cut their taunts short, and smile at her.

Because of this, Smelly Shirley liked me and once asked me into her home for tea. I accepted but was almost sick when I went there. It did smell and I really didn't want to drink the cup of tea she handed me. Yet, that day, I realized that behind the filth was a lovely human being and, afterwards, I was always extra nice to Smelly Shirley. Being kind to her just felt like the right thing to do.

Now, she was floating above my bed.

'I spent my time on earth,' she said. 'It's time to leave. I'm dying, Joe, but I wanted to thank you and say goodbye.'

I was touched. The next morning I called several people in Skelmersdale, but nobody wanted to go and check up on her. I drove home that Saturday and went straight to Shirley's house. The curtains were closed so I went next door to my mate Paddy's house.

'Shirley died on Thursday,' Paddy told me. That was the day she had visited me. 'The doctors amputated her leg, but infection had set in and the poison invaded her body. She died at home.'

I was sadder for the life she had lived than for her death. So many people had ridiculed her over the years. It must have been a difficult existence. Through my work, I was learning that some people are somehow out of place during their time on earth and need extra understanding and kindness.

*

On one occasion, when I was back in Ormskirk between classes at Arthur Findlay College, I went to the shops and bought two expensive Lacroix jumpers. I finally had some money from all the readings I had been doing, and it felt good to earn a living doing what I had trained to do my entire life.

That night, in a dream, I saw a glass carriage. It was right out of the nineteenth century. I recognized it as a hearse and, as the carriage drew closer, the driver introduced himself as Giles. He pointed at my new jumpers. I freaked out and woke up. Did the vision of the hearse mean I was going to die? I was so frightened I checked out some life-insurance policies and made a quick will, leaving what I had to my children. I also gave away the new sweaters to a man on the street. The spirit world probably got a hearty laugh over the drama I made out of the whole thing.

Three days later, the undertaker returned in a dream. He drew the carriage up alongside me and once again said that his name was Giles.

'I'm not here to take you away,' he chuckled. 'I'm back because I scared you awake the other night.'

Giles told me he was part of my new spirit team. 'My job is to help people get in touch with you on the other side to give messages to their families.' Now, in my more advanced state, he was part of the team.

Giles became a true teacher and helper. During stage performances, he would park his spiritual carriage on the stage, and it would light up with 'Mum' or 'Grandfather' so I could identify who the visitor was straight away.

I was extremely grateful to all my spirit guides, including that rascal Ruby.

Claudine continued to get me coverage in British magazines and newspapers. Laura Kendall, a journalist with a local London newspaper, *The Wharf*, asked me to work on a feature with her. The paper was distributed around Docklands, in the East End, where Jack the Ripper had stalked his victims.

I had never been to that part of London, but Laura asked me to walk around the East End to see what spirits would show me. The first spirit that came was a Chinese man who said he had murdered his wife.

'That's amazing,' Laura said. 'This is London's old Chinatown.'

I went on, picking up energies in various locations as we walked.

During this exercise, two of London's most notorious gangsters appeared to me. Reggie and Ronnie Kray were identical twins who pretty much controlled the East End in the 1950s and 1960s. They were involved in murders, violent assaults, armed robberies, arson, even torture, and owned plush nightclubs which counted Hollywood royalty among their clientele. The twins hobnobbed with stars such as Frank Sinatra, Judy Garland and Diana Dors, and gained a level of prestige alongside their success in organized crime.

Police caught up with them in 1968 and, at the age of thirty-five, the brothers were put in prison for the rest of their lives. A massive heart attack killed Ronnie in 1995.

Reggie died in 2000 at the age of sixty-seven, having lived almost half his life behind bars, separated from the other prisoners.

Now, their spirits were standing on the very streets they used to rule over. I was shocked. Why were these two famous mobsters coming to me?

'You were a criminal once too,' Ronnie told me. 'You understand.'

'This was our turf,' Reggie said. 'We owned this part of London. You're on our patch.'

I had no idea how to tell Laura and convince her that what I was saying was true. 'Give me some proof that you're here,' I said in my mind to the brothers.

'Tell the reporter someone else was supposed to join you today. His fingers are missing.'

'What a strange message,' I thought, but I relayed it to Laura.

Her face flushed. 'The photographer was supposed to be here to take pictures,' she said.

Had he had an accident and done some damage to his fingers? I didn't want to think about it.

We rounded the next corner and were both taken aback when we ran into the cameraman: he was wearing fingerless gloves.

That convinced Laura that the Krays were indeed in our presence. She'd been a sceptic when we met but, because of the information that came through with the Chinese man and the details about the Krays, she wrote in her article that there was something to my work; it was uncanny.

After that first meeting, the Krays continued to visit me in my flat. I was fascinated to know how the two most flagrant mobsters in England had transitioned to the other side. They told me they were back with their mother, Violet, who had idolized the twins on earth. Even though she had been aware of their corruption, she had always welcomed them home and covered up for their crimes.

'We were wrong on earth,' Ronnie confided in me. 'We've given up crime and are making peace with our victims.' He went on to say that some of their victims had forgiven them but others had not. 'We wasted way too many years rotting in prison. I was highly intelligent and thought I'd made a great name for myself. But, in prison, I felt like a mug. All our violence on earth was wrong.'

'We have started a new chapter on this side,' Reggie said. 'People over here see that we've changed and that we want to be honest. Ambition is still part of our character and personality, but now we'll be Reggie and Ronnie in a positive way.'

While the twins were enjoying their freedom, mixing with other spirits, Ronnie met up with a former girlfriend who had committed suicide. 'We are mending the hurt and enjoy getting reacquainted,' he said. Now Ronnie assists troubled children on earth, urging them to stay out of gangs. He is using his earthly knowledge to help kids in the same situation he was in on earth.

While I was writing this book, the Kray brothers visited me again. They said they would return to earth in 150 years' time. Meanwhile, they are making peace on the other side and preparing to build a positive incarnation on earth in the future.

The Kray visit opened me up to a whole new world of mobsters. I was called to a house in Maghull, a suburb of Liverpool, to perform a private reading for four women. I settled myself at the kitchen table with the first woman, and her father came through. Suddenly, I heard a commotion in the living room. The home-owner's son had come home and was furious that I was in the house.

'He's a conman,' the son insisted. 'I'll have him give me a reading and prove he's full of shit.'

The guy was a hulking six-foot-three, with bulging arms and a huge, bald head. He sat down in front of me, and I immediately felt a bad vibe. Two young men in spirit stood beside him. I shared this with the man in front of me and relayed some information they gave me. 'They tell me you are competing in a weightlifting competition in three weeks' time.'

'How did you know that?'

Both men flashed a vision, and I knew they had been shot. 'Do you know two men who were shot?'

His eyes rounded into full moons. He had two friends who had been shot dead at the gym.

'These men say you have just bought a farm,' I said. 'It's dangerous. You need to get out of the deal.'

The man almost fainted. He had bought the farm that very day.

'Your friends are talking about drugs and say you need to move in a different direction with your life.'

Some time later, the man called me to say that he had sold the farm, which he had been going to use for his drug business. He was starting on a new path.

After these incidents, I received a flood of phone calls from members of the criminal underworld. Some people who had called came to my flat for readings. One guy named Peter had killed a gangster named Gary, who showed up in spirit at the reading.

Peter was totally shaken up by it; the tears were streaming down his face and I thought he might collapse. Peter told me he had served fourteen years for the murder and had been released just that week. 'What is he saying?' Peter was shaking visibly now.

'He wants you to know that he forgives you.'

Peter cradled his face in his hands and cried like a baby.

Gary told me that, even though Peter had taken his life, he had watched him in prison all those years and seen that he was extremely remorseful for what he had done and had asked Gary many times for forgiveness.

Peter was very grateful for Gary's kind message and, once again, I was amazed at how healing this kind of interaction with spirit could be.

Recently, a man telephoned and offered to pay me twice my usual fee if I could come straight away and assist his family with an emergency. I was called to a farm on the outskirts of Liverpool and could barely believe it when I was buzzed through an electronic gate to find a whole array of cars, jeeps and trucks from Manchester and London parked outside. Instantly, a headline from the

Liverpool Echo flashed into my mind. I recognized it as the headline from the day before. A big-time drug dealer had been shot and killed. This meeting had to have something to do with that. It was like being in a movie about the Mafia.

I was scared when I went in. I was gestured to take a seat among a mob of high-powered gangsters. They told me that one of their own, a guy named Shawn, had been shot to death. He was a drug dealer and had lived in the country. His mates wanted me to find out who had killed him.

Shawn came through immediately and tried to identify his murderer.

Ruby stepped in and said, 'Joe, you are putting your life in danger. Do not go that far. Talk about what Shawn is doing on the other side.' Ruby explained that the mobsters were out for revenge and would retaliate by killing whoever had shot Shawn. I couldn't allow them to exploit me into leading them to murder.

I stopped Shawn from relaying the name and shared only a positive message for his family. He said he was concerned for his girlfriend and children.

'He says your family and friends are working on a joint venture to build a hotel,' I told them. 'Shawn said to proceed with that and put up a plaque in his name.'

About a week later, I was called to another house to see four people there. Shawn came through again. 'Tell my son I'm okay, and don't get involved,' he said. 'I love him and miss him.'

I was surprised to learn that this was Shawn's son's

home. The son was amazed and very pleased to hear from his dad.

'Bury me in my white suit,' Shawn said. 'I wish I could have said goodbye on earth.' His funeral was scheduled for the following week.

Another time, a man I'll call Jerry came to me for a reading after his friend had been shot and killed at a local gym. Jerry was a burly fellow and was involved with the criminal underworld. His friend came through in spirit and offered information.

'You must be doing something in the security business,' I shared with Jerry. 'Be careful when you drive and leave your home, because someone is planning to shoot you.'

Jerry looked frightened.

'Did you upset somebody?' I asked. 'Do you know a Kevin?'

Jerry nodded.

'There is something to do with property. Don't get involved with the deal.'

Jerry almost fell over. 'I was just talking to Kevin today about some property,' he said.

Jerry continued to come to me for readings and thanked me for helping him out of a dangerous situation. In actual fact, it was the spirit world that had provided the information. I was just the messenger.

'You have a good spirit and soul and need to change direction,' I relayed. 'Don't ride the crime and greed conveyor belt with all your mates.'

Several weeks later, Jerry called me to the gym, where he was feeling a frightening energy. He picked me up in a big Land Rover and drove me there. I immediately determined that the energy was that of one of Jerry's friends, who had been murdered.

'He came here to let you know he is okay on the other side,' I said. 'He wants to say goodbye. He's not a negative energy; he was just trying to get your attention. He is not haunting the place, just trying to communicate.'

He was very grateful for my help, and I was pleased to be able to give it – to him and to others. Helen McCourt's mother, Marie, continued to invite me to SAMM meetings. People with murdered loved ones were eager to connect with them through me. Sons, daughters, sisters and brothers came through at these gatherings, and the accuracy of the information I was able to relay continued to impress.

My guides helped tremendously at the SAMM meetings, especially Giles, who lit up his carriage to announce the next arrival.

These sessions provided great comfort and relief for people who had once been destroyed by their loss. It allowed many people to resume their own lives, knowing that their loved ones were happy and healthy on the other side. I found being able to pass on messages like these profoundly rewarding, and it reinforced my belief in the meaning of my work.

15

After Laura Kendall's article appeared in *The Wharf*, magazines began contacting me to write predictions in their publications. These were interesting requests, and I wanted to explore them. How does the spirit world know what will happen in the future and how would I be able to access that information?

I asked my wonderful spirit teacher, Arthur Findlay, and he told me that the spirit world operates ten years ahead of earth time so the spirits who visit mediums can see the future. This really caught my interest, so I decided to test it out.

Fate and Fortune magazine gave me a column for my predictions and, as I sat down to try this form of mediumship, Sharon Osbourne's deceased mother came through.

'Sharon is about to land a talk show on television,' she told me.

At the time, Sharon was a judge on the wildly popular *X-Factor*. 'Sharon will have an on-air blow-out with a finalist,' her mother told me.

Astoundingly, both these things happened.

Princess Diana came through another time, and told me to expect more headlines and scandal surrounding her fatal car crash. She told me that the cameras had not been working in the tunnel where the accident occurred. Sure enough, conspiracy theories on Diana's tragic death have dominated the news for years.

A spirit family member of famous football player Wayne Rooney told me that he would have two operations on his foot. This also happened.

With help from my spirit teachers, I predicted that a public outcry would force managers to rehire football great David Beckham, and this, too, turned out to be correct.

My guides told me that Saddam Hussein's own people would execute him. I saw him hanging. This was before his trial and conviction.

I also predicted, with help from my vital spirit sources, that Gordon Brown would become prime minister and bring some British troops home in 2007.

The feedback I got on these predictions was amazing. The editor even wrote an article praising me in the magazine. It was a good training exercise for me, because I realized that I had been doing predictions all along with my regular readings. The guides were showing me that using my mediumship to read celebrities and sports heroes was no different to doing readings for anyone else. It took away the intimidation factor.

Well, almost. I started receiving visits from members of the royal family. I didn't seek this out, and indeed tried to stop it, but with no success. The Queen Mother came through to say that she was with Diana in the spirit world and that she wanted all the conspiracy theories over Diana's death to stop, because they were harming

Diana's sons. I was embarrassed. What on earth was I supposed to do with this information? Call the Queen? But the royal spirits continued to come.

My guides explained that the royals were only spiritual souls like everybody else. My teachers wanted me to aim higher and to trust that my ability worked in exactly the same way for every level of society, from the Queen to a homeless man on the street.

This allowed me to relax a little when I did a reading for 1960s rock star David Essex. His first visitor was none other than John Lennon! I didn't want to make myself appear ridiculous by voicing this, but John Lennon was standing right in front of me.

I cleared my throat and stated firmly, 'John Lennon is here, and he says you two have a connection in the United States.'

David laughed. 'We did once meet in America, and Lennon offered me a ride to get away from the paparazzi.'

That was not the last I would see and hear from the legendary Beatle.

In 2006, Paul Sharratt of Starcast Productions in Los Angeles contacted Claudine. He was researching mediums in the UK and wanted someone with an excellent reputation to psychically contact John Lennon.

The same production company had produced the controversial show, *The Spirit of Diana*, in 2003. The show created quite a stir in the United Kingdom. Now, Paul told me, he wanted to produce a similar show, called *The Spirit of John Lennon*. He explained that the Lennon show would be filmed in the same style, with a séance featuring a medium and, hopefully, John Lennon's spirit as the guest of honour.

I told Paul I had already met Lennon during the David Essex reading, so I knew I would have no problem contacting him again. Paul had me do readings for a few of their producers over the phone. My information, and the accuracy of it, impressed them, so they asked me to be the medium on the show.

I needed Lennon's permission and to ask if he wanted to appear on the show, so I contacted him in my flat.

'Yoko won't like it,' John said.

'Does that mean no?'

'I say, let's go for it,' John said.

I was still afraid of one thing. 'You're so popular, and so much has been written about you. How will people believe I am in contact with you?'

Suddenly, the lights started flashing in my living room. I heard a voice say out loud, 'Trust me!'

I was still a bit sceptical and concerned, but I signed a contract with Starcast Productions to do the show. It would be my first trip to America. What was I getting myself into?

Initially, the Los Angeles crew flew to Liverpool to film me in and around John Lennon's old stomping ground. I was a perfect match for the show since I was also from Liverpool and could communicate the atmosphere of the area. It took a while, but I started to feel relaxed on camera and was able to allow John's energy to guide me to visit several locations. First, I was drawn into a hair salon, where I strongly felt strong John and the other Beatles' presence.

The hairdresser nodded and said that John had often stopped in for a haircut. I had a vision of there being Beatles pictures above the ceiling. It seemed odd, but the hairdresser confirmed that there was a storage space above the dropped ceiling. Years before, the Beatles had signed pictures which had hung in the salon.

'They could very well still be up there,' the hairdresser said.

Our next stop was the Cavern Club, where the Beatles famously performed. As I walked down the black steps, the camera rolling, I sensed mania and women screaming for the singer.

I heard John shout, 'Eddie Cochran.'

As I continued down the stairs, deeper into the Cavern, I heard 1960s music blaring. 'I hear the name McFall and the initial R. Was it Roy or Ray?' I said to the camera. Now I was visualizing John picking up his guitar.

'He says this is where he played.'

I was drawn to the bar, where I asked the bartender about a guy named McFall.

'A Ray McFall was the second owner of the Cavern.' The bartender also told me that Eddie Cochran had performed there.

The camera then followed me into Quarry Bank School, which John had attended up to the age of fifteen. As I walked up the stairs, I felt John's mischievous energy running up those same steps.

'I used to sneak alcohol in here and smoke cigarettes,' John told me, and I shared the information on camera. 'We named my first group The Quarrymen after this school. I didn't care about schoolwork. I recognized my passion for music at an early age, and it became my sole interest.'

Next, we visited the Jacaranda Club. Elvis Presley, Buddy Holly and Chuck Berry all influenced John's early music. He told me the young Quarrymen had performed here, but only over a brief period of time.

George Harrison's spirit stepped in and told me the group had sparred with their first manager, Allan Williams.

'I see a vision ... blue. Is it a band?' I said to the camera. 'I hear "angel, angel, angel". John is quite happy, but he didn't really get to say goodbye properly to Allan. He wants to say it now. We are all friends, he says.'

Later, the show's producer interviewed Allan Williams. He confirmed that he had had a row with John over his commission and John had let him go.

'I told John he was getting big-headed,' Allan said on the show. 'I told him he would never work again, but it was me who never worked again.'

Allan said he told John that the Beatles was a silly name for the group and had suggested Long John Silver instead. They had settled on the Silver Beatles, and Allan still has copies of contracts with the group under that name.

He also mentioned that he had owned a club called the Blue Angels, where the Beatles had played. It was popular because it had a licence to sell alcohol, and the women, in particular, were keen on the music that was played there.

'John had a king-sized chip on his shoulder,' Allan said, 'but he was a very nice person underneath.'

After shooting in Liverpool, I was dissatisfied. Everything John had shared with me was already public knowledge.

I was in for a bigger shock when I learned that Starcast Productions was planning to air the show on pay-per-view. The media considered pay-per-view as little better than a way of raising money, but I felt comfortable enough with making the show because I had John Lennon's permission and trusted him. I had also been impressed with Paul Sharratt and his crew, who insisted that the show be authentic and not contrived or hyped. That was the only way I could work with them.

After taping around Liverpool, we flew to New York City, where Paul and I appeared on *Showbiz Tonight*, a national entertainment-news programme on CNN. The interview was typical of the mainstream media. The host, A. J. Hammer, was polite, but he gave the interview a typical sceptic's slant.

'A lot of people say the whole idea of psychics is a bunch of nonsense,' Hammer said. 'What do you say to those people?'

'Everyone has their own opinion,' I replied. 'If people don't have any experience of an afterlife, they may not believe, but that is still just their perception. It's only one opinion.'

Even though Paul, the executive producer of *The Spirit of John Lennon*, was himself a sceptic, he told the host that John Lennon and Princess Diana were both spiritual people and had believed in an afterlife.

'This show is 100 per cent genuine.'

As the interview wound down, I felt a tap on my shoulder. I heard Lennon say, 'Quick, before the interview ends ... I'm going to show up during the séance.'

This put me in a huge quandary. Here I was on live television, beaming into living rooms all over America. The séance was still a week away. How would I handle this? Suddenly, I blurted out that I was quite confident that John would come through.

'I'm hoping we'll catch him on film,' I said to A. J. Hammer. 'He wants to come through. I always ask permission beforehand.'

'What will we see?' Hammer asked.

'This might be a big night. We could see his spirit, or him coming close with his energy.'

After the interview, my stomach lurched. I had just told millions of Americans that John Lennon would show up at the séance. I was nervous about it, but still had faith that it would happen. No other medium had ever made such a prediction on US television.

The show's producers had arranged for the séance to take place at the La Fortuna Café in New York City. John and Yoko had frequented the place because it was close to the Dakota, the apartment building where they lived. I was happy to meet La Fortuna's owner, Vincent Urwand, whom Lennon had affectionately called Uncle Vinny.

Vinny showed us to the table where John and Yoko ate when they visited the café. I took a seat at this table with Uncle Vinny, and his nephew Mike Trapani, who now runs La Fortuna. Also joining us were Curtis Pollock and Gwen Frey, John Lennon devotees.

Before we started, I told John that I needed information that was not public knowledge in order for these Lennon experts to believe that John was really there in spirit. We lit white candles, lowered the lights and all placed our hands palms down on the round table.

'When I do a séance, I may go into a semi-trance state, but I still know what's going on,' I told the participants on camera. 'My voice may alter slightly, but do not be concerned.

'John is coming closer and he just kissed Vinny on the head saying, "It's been a long time." John is very excited. He is telling me something about your ears or your hearing,' I said to Vinny.

'My ears are about the only good thing left on me,' Vinny chuckled.

I was angry at John. In my mind I told him he'd better come up with something else.

John laughed. 'Tell Vinny about the old jukebox.'

Vinny said the jukebox had been a birthday gift from Yoko, the last present she had bought for John before he was shot. 'Nobody knew this,' Vinny said. 'I bought John the old 78s to put in it.'

John told me Vinny had had a heart-bypass operation, and Vinny confirmed this.

I allowed the participants to ask questions, and Curtis wanted to know if John regretted that the Beatles never got back together.

'Yes, in a way, but it wasn't meant to be. We had our time, and Yoko and I went our own way. There were arguments in the end. It just wasn't the same. They are still special people in my heart, and we will always be the Beatles.'

Vinny asked if John approved of the changes that had been made in the café over the years since his death.

'He approves of everything,' I relayed. 'John is getting emotional, with tears of happiness and joy. He is saying, "Thank you, Vinny, and your family, for keeping the café going. I don't want you to worry about a thing."'

'What advice does John have for today's generation?' Curtis asked.

'Wisdom and knowledge. Know the world is in pain. John is pointing to the famine and to the children dying in Africa. He wants help to come through music. He is still anti-war.'

'Would he rather be remembered for peace or his music?'

'Peace and music. Music is peace. Murder is senseless.'

At the end of the evening, I was still not satisfied with the information I had received from John. The information about the jukebox was the only thing that had previously not been known, but was that enough? Why hadn't John shown up, as he had promised to? And I had announced to an entire nation on live television that he would.

After the shoot, I was sitting in the production van when I heard a loud shout: 'Everyone re-gather around the table!' It turned out that my microphone had stopped working during a short part of the séance. Audio technicians Luciano Dias and Michael Fronberg had checked the soundtrack on the camera and were stunned at what they'd heard.

On the tape, when my microphone had gone dead, there was a clear message. 'Peace ... peace ... peace. The message is peace.'

'This has never happened before,' Michael said. 'It was on Joe's soundtrack. We switched to Vinny's, but it didn't pick up the message. Nobody was speaking those words when we were taping. We checked all four cameras. We cannot edit in the field, and we don't have special effects on our cameras. I cannot explain what happened, but the message is beautiful.'

We were all absolutely flabbergasted at the emotion-filled voice and message, and I was especially pleased that this portion of the programme had been live.

I had already been aware of EVP, or Electronic Voice Phenomena. Spirits can form words from electronic white noise. The show's producers took the recording to Sandra Belanger, an anthropologist and EVP expert. She declared that John's peace message was a Class-A EVP, which means it is clearly audible without headphones.

My intentions for *The Spirit of John Lennon* were pure and in keeping with John's wishes. I am probably the first medium in the world to have made a prediction that John Lennon would come through.

He did, and I was very grateful that he kept his word, helping others understand that we're all spiritual souls who never really die.

16

In January 2006, another famous murder victim came to me in my flat. Eighteen-year-old Sally Anne Bowman had been murdered outside her home on 25 September the year before. She told me she wanted me to get in touch with her mother, Linda, and the police to help find her killer.

Sally Anne had worked as a hairdresser and had partied with her sister the night her body was found on her driveway with blood pooling from seven stab wounds. She had also been bitten and raped. Three of the wounds were so deep that they went through her torso and came out of her back.

'I know the killer,' Sally Anne told me. She sent me a vision of the murderer and showed him working with food and catering. As I smelled the pungent odour of cooking onions, I sensed he worked as a chef in hotels and pubs. I also saw him working at weddings and other functions, where he first noticed some of his victims. Sally Anne said he had committed rape before.

She gave the names of family members and friends and shared her personal interests. She had been an aspiring model at the time of her murder and not long before had been signed by a top modelling agency. I wrote up several pages of notes from Sally Anne's visit, and Claudine emailed them to the Metropolitan Police.

I told the police that the killer's name was Mark and that he had been to Holland. Sally Anne showed me that there was some kind of an issue over a football game. These two facts made no sense to me, but I included them for the police.

'Your sketch of the killer in the national newspaper is wrong,' I wrote in the email I sent. Sally Anne had shown me her murderer, and the e-fit was inaccurate.

The next day, Claudine received an email from Detective Gerry Douglas.

'I have taken up your kind offer to ask Joe a few questions, which I hope he will be able to assist with,' he wrote. The email requested specific information from Sally Anne about the flats she had mentioned. He also wanted identifying landmarks to help with the search, and a description of the killer's vehicle – whether it was a car or a bicycle.

We emailed back and forth, and a meeting was set up, through a reporter at the *Croydon Advertiser* office, with Sally Anne's mother, Linda, her sister, Sally Anne's boyfriend, Lewis, and the police family-liaison officer who had been assigned to be in communication with the Bowmans until the killer was caught.

We met for ninety minutes in a reporter's office. Linda did not want information from this meeting to appear in the newspaper, so the reporter was not in the room. I tried very hard to get Sally Anne through, but the atmosphere was not right. Linda and her other daughter were still in a state of shock over the murder. Energy from others at a reading, and even the setting, can interfere with communication. Sometimes I will pick up wrong information from someone else in the room. Only parts of Sally Anne's clues made sense.

'Now your daughter is showing me only white,' I said. 'I don't know if it's a name or a colour, or the name of a place. Does that make any sense, Linda?'

Linda remained silent.

On another occasion, Sally Anne visited me again and told me the killer had a little boy. I shared this information with the police, too. Soon after, in June, I had another meeting with Linda. Linda's friend Paula and the liaison officer were also present at this second meeting. Sally Anne came through and wished her mother a happy birthday.

'Your daughter is showing me a caravan, a white transit van, a burgundy car and a pile of towels.' I was confused.

'Lloyd Road!' Sally Anne shouted. 'Ask Mum where she went for her birthday.'

'The Jack and Jill pub,' Linda said. Amazingly, it was on Lloyd Road.

'The killer is connected to this establishment or some area with food,' I said.

Linda's mouth dropped open, and the officer started to write like crazy.

'Sally Anne wants me to mention the money box and fifty pence.'

Linda told me that the police had taken this box and money from Sally Anne's house.

Sally Anne described an area with tennis courts and gypsy caravans and said it was on Lloyd Road, about four or five miles from Linda's house. She kept on about her mother's birthday night and said that it was on the same date as the killer's birthday.

The information was so compelling that we decided to drive out to the Jack and Jill pub to see if I could pick up any more there. On the drive there, I had a vision of a man sitting in the pub with beads around his neck.

'The name Steven is important,' Sally Anne told me. Next, she showed me a flash picture of a satchel. Again, I was confused.

As we drew close to the pub, I could not believe my eyes when I spotted this same satchel resting against the front door on somebody's porch. I swung into the drive, and Linda, Paula and I sneaked up to the door and looked inside the bag. It contained some clothes, but we heard someone coming and hurried away. We did not want to come face to face with the killer.

Then, when we pulled into the car park at the Jack and Jill pub, I was amazed to find a white van and a burgundy car. Towels were piled in the window, just as I had seen in the vision. I knew we were in the right place. I was certain the killer hung about in this area.

Inside the pub, Linda called the police so that they could check the number plate on the burgundy car. They questioned someone connected to the van, but it was the wrong man. I knew the vehicles in the car park were only a reference so that I would recognize the correct spot. I figured the satchel was also a reference. In the pub, my eyes almost popped out of my head: there was a man sitting in a booth in the pub with beads around his neck – more proof.

Before we were able to fit the pieces of the puzzle together, the police arrested Mark Dixie, right next to the Jack and Jill pub. It turned out that Dixie had been arrested a week earlier in a fight over a football match. At that time, the police had taken a routine DNA sample which, on testing, matched genetic material found at the scene of Sally Anne's murder. That explained Sally Anne's clue about the perpetrator having some connection with a football match.

Later, Dixie admitted he had been celebrating his thirty-fifth birthday the evening of Sally Anne's murder. He had spent the night at a friend's flat near her house. He was high on alcohol and cocaine when he attacked and killed Sally Anne on her driveway then raped her dead body.

Mark Dixie had worked at various hotels serving food. He wore a white chef's coat, which explained Sally Anne's reference to white. He had recently returned from Holland where he had been hiding after Sally Anne's murder. His girlfriend had just had a baby boy. It was later revealed in the press that many of Mark Dixie's friends knew him under different names, and one of these aliases was Steven MacDonald, which explained why Sally Anne had told me the name Steven was important.

As usual, I was floored at the accuracy of the spirit

victim's puzzle-piece clues. Later, Mark Dixie was questioned about unsolved murders in Australia, and was under suspicion of being a serial killer.

The case of three-month-old Shannon Cunningham was one of the most emotionally difficult cases I have worked on. A criminal justice firm hired me to help determine who killed her.

Shannon's father, Scott Cunningham, was already in prison awaiting trial for the murder, but his family thought that Shannon's mother, Shelley Wright, was the killer and had retained private investigators in the hope that they could prove Scott innocent.

Scott, his girlfriend Shelley and baby Shannon were living with Scott's uncle, Colin Cunningham, when the baby died. The private investigators, Rob and Steve, took me to the uncle's house to see if I could pick up any vibes, feelings or thoughts. They asked me to recreate what had happened that night. I insisted that no members of the family attend my walk-through in order that their thoughts and energies would not influence me. I needed a clear mind and conscience to proceed. Only Rob, Steve and Claudine entered the house, bringing a tape recorder to capture what I felt and learned.

They took me into what looked like a living room. 'This room used to have a bed. Scott and Shelley lived in this room,' Rob said.

I had an immediate vision of Scott purposely dropping the infant. I sensed it was not the first time. In fact, Scott had physically hurt the baby during the couple of weeks before her death. I asked everyone to leave the room so I could concentrate alone.

I psychically saw the couple watching a football game. Scott left to prepare the baby's bottle. Now I saw Shelley making sandwiches, and both were in the kitchen. I smelled alcohol and sensed Scott was jealous and thought his uncle was carrying on with Shelley.

Next, I saw Shelley leave the house and smoke a cigarette in the garden. Scott picked up baby Shannon. I felt the baby dropping and knew she was winded and could no longer cry. I psychically witnessed Scott hitting the child, then I heard an enormous, sickening thud. The baby was hit in the head with some kind of weapon. I saw blood on the kitchen walls, floor and ceiling.

The gruesome playback was horrendous to witness. I watched Scott washing blood off the baby's head in the kitchen sink. My heart cried out for that tiny little girl, who had no way to protect herself from her savage father.

The private investigators were shocked to hear what I had seen. They had been certain I would implicate Shannon's mother, Shelley. Shelley had told the police she'd been asleep on the bed when Scott woke her.

'What have you done?' he cried.

She looked over and saw her dead daughter on the bed beside her.

After my scan of the house, Scott's parents, with Colin and two friends, entered, anxious for me to tell them that their son was innocent.

'I'm not prepared to offer any information at the

moment,' I said. The reality was too brutal and raw in my mind to tell them point blank. 'I will only say that the culprit buried a weapon in the garden and threw something over the back fence.'

The family became excited, thinking they would finally have evidence against Shelley. The relatives searched for the weapon, but the bushes were too tall and dense. They were pleased, and hopeful that I had resolved the case in Scott's favour.

The family asked if I wanted to meet with Scott himself in Parkhurst Prison, one of the highest-security prisons in England. It was intriguing going with the private investigators to meet this baby killer face to face. The thought of his crime made me feel sick.

As soon as I shook his hand, I had a vision of him battering the baby. As if it were a video recording playing in my head, I felt as if I were inside his mind. Every time he looked at his daughter's face, he saw Shelley. He hated his girlfriend and transferred this rage to their three-month-old child. This was the first time I had ever got a motive for a murder. This went beyond who had killed baby Shannon. I watched the psychic video of Scott glaring at the baby with disgust because she looked like Shelley.

'If you're a psychic, tell me the nickname I had for Shannon,' Scott said.

I decided to play a psychological game with him. 'I'm here to help you get off this murder you did not commit,' I taunted. Something inside me was guiding me to handle the situation in this way. 'You're in real trouble here.

There were five people in that house and, obviously, you're innocent.'

I was totally startled by what I heard next. Shannon's spirit was now in the room. 'Daddy killed me.'

I wanted to bash Scott's head in. Instead, I remained calm. 'Scott, tell me everything that happened that night.'

'I was watching the football game with Uncle Colin.'

'What was Shelley doing?'

'She was in the kitchen preparing bottles.'

'What next?'

'I had a few drinks.'

'What was Shelley doing?'

'She was just coming in and out of the room. The baby started to cry, so I picked her up and walked back to the room where we had been watching the football game, but Uncle Colin had gone to bed.'

Suddenly, I had a terrifying vision of Scott dropping baby Shannon.

'I put the baby back in the cot,' Scott continued, 'and went out to the garden to have a cigarette with Shelley.'

'What happened next?'

'I went to the kitchen to make a sandwich and cut my finger on the cheese grater, and it bled.'

'Keep going.'

'I fell asleep. Later, I woke up and was going to check on the baby. I found her lying on the bed next to Shelley. Shannon was covered with blood. I screamed at Shelley and asked what she had done.'

I saw flashes of the baby killed in the kitchen, then

Scott bringing her to the bathroom, where he washed more blood off her face.

'Why did you wake up? If it was dark, how did you see that the baby was injured?'

Scott started to clam up, and his eyes filled with tears.

'Tell me who you think killed Shannon,' I said.

I knew he was backed into a corner.

'I think it was Uncle Colin.'

'Why Colin?'

'I don't know. I think he wanted us out of the house.'

I later learned why Scott changed his story about Shelley killing the baby: the police had found Uncle Colin's blood in the kitchen drain as well as Shannon's. Colin Cunningham was innocent. He suffered from nosebleeds, which explained why his blood was in the drain.

I felt like a cop. I knew he was lying through his teeth. 'Scott, I know the killer used a weapon. The only way we can get you out of this prison is to know what that murder weapon was. Unless we can locate this weapon, you face twenty-five years behind bars. Can you think of anything that could have been used and where it could possibly be?'

The autopsy had shown that Shannon's tiny skull had been staved in and extensively fractured. The coroner said he had never seen a baby with so many injuries, including multiple bruises, a fractured jaw, collarbone and several ribs. Scott's blood-alcohol level that night was more than three times the legal limit for driving.

'The only thing I can think of are the glass candlesticks. They're heavy and thick. Ask my mother about them, because she packed my stuff away.'

'Okay, we'll get the candlesticks, to see if they were what was used.'

Outside the prison, I met with Scott's father, but there was no way I could tell him his son had murdered his own baby. I kept thinking of Shannon saying, 'Daddy killed me.'

We went straight to Scott's parents' house, where the bed was now in a spare room for guests to use. I lay on the bed and had a sickening vision of Scott battering the baby for weeks before she died.

While I was lying on the bed, a man in spirit came through. He told me his name was Wayne and that he had committed suicide. He was Scott's brother.

'Scott killed the baby,' Wayne said. 'Don't speak to him.'

I had had no idea before this that Scott had had a brother who committed suicide, but his mother confirmed it when I went downstairs.

We returned to Colin's house to search for the candlesticks. His mother went up to the loft and brought down the candlesticks Scott had described. We noticed a chip missing from the bottom of one of them and what looked like blood. The private investigators had them forensically tested, and found that it wasn't blood, but began testing for DNA.

I wrote up a final report for the investigators, and they were utterly shocked and sickened that baby Shannon's killer was pleading innocent. I let Rob and Steve break the news to the family.

Scott Cunningham was convicted of Shannon's murder

and sentenced to life in prison. Shelley was not charged. Scott's family is still fighting to get him out.

This case was extremely difficult for me, since it involved a helpless infant. I also realized that I had put my own life at risk by sitting with the family. But I also learned to follow my instincts and enter these situations with a clear mind.

I was fascinated that I had entered Scott's auric field, which stores history, and, for the first time, learned the motive for a murder. I had tapped into this information without him knowing it, and followed my own intuition and guidance in dealing with this killer one on one.

In March 2008, the case of a missing nine-year-old girl from Dewsbury made national news in England. Shannon Matthews had disappeared on her way home from a school swimming trip on 19 February, and her mother was frantic to find her.

The search for Shannon exploded into Britain's biggest-ever missing-person search, with six hundred officers assigned to the case.

Shannon's mother, Karen, made numerous public appeals and television appearances, pleading for her 'princess' to return home. The plight of this precious girl gripped the country, reminded of the hunt for missing four-year-old Madeleine McCann.

The editor of the *People* newspaper contacted Claudine to ask if I had worked on Shannon's case. When Claudine said no, the newspaper asked me to help, so I went to the area near her school where she was last seen. A *People* reporter, Simon Lennon, joined me and audio-recorded everything I said. I was drawn to a nearby hairdresser, where I sensed her abductor had been hanging about.

'I feel Shannon got into a car with someone she knew,' I said.

After that, Simon and I met with Shannon's mother and her boyfriend, Craig Meehan, at their house. The two seemed a bit nervous when I told them what I had seen surrounding Shannon's abduction. At one point, Craig looked so uncomfortable with my information that he got up and left the room.

'Maybe he should stay,' I told Karen. 'Do you know a Mick or Michael? He's connected with Craig.'

Karen wagged her head but could barely maintain eye contact with me.

'I keep hearing the name Paul. I feel this person is a relative.'

Now Karen anxiously rose and followed Craig into the kitchen.

The whole situation seemed somehow odd, but I couldn't figure out why the parents seemed so nervous. I picked up that there was something related to Craig on the computer.

Karen returned to the living room and handed me Shannon's favourite Bratz shirt, which I clutched in my hands.

Suddenly, little Keith Bennett, the lad who was murdered and buried on the moors, appeared. 'She's been taken to Batley,' he said.

'This is someone quite close to your family. I'm pretty

convinced you know this person,' I told Karen. I continued to hear the name Paul and psychically saw Shannon sitting on his knee at a funeral. She knew this person as a family friend.

Claudine sent an email to the police with this information and also mentioned that the initial 'D' was important. Also, she mentioned that I had visualized the abductor driving a car and visiting a church near some arches with Shannon.

Six days later, Claudine screamed when television networks broke into programming to announce that the police had found Shannon Matthews alive.

The reporter from the *People* contacted me immediately. 'I just listened to the recording of your reading with Karen, and it was so accurate,' he said.

Detectives had broken down the door of a home in Batley and found Shannon hidden in the base of a bed. They also discovered thirty-nine-year-old Mick Donovan, who also went by the name of Paul Drake, hiding under another bed in the room. The 'D' was for both last names!

It turned out that Donovan was Craig Meehan's uncle. Witnesses confirmed that Shannon had sat on his lap at Craig's father's recent funeral.

The Shannon Matthews case took several more shocking twists. Her abductor was remanded in jail and charged with kidnapping and imprisonment. Behind bars, he took pills and slit his wrists, but doctors saved him.

The police found more than a hundred child-porn pictures on Craig Meehan's computer, and arrested him too. That explained my vision of Craig's computer.

I also learned why Shannon's mother, Karen, had been so uncomfortable around me. She broke down to her family liaison officer and reportedly admitted that she had known where Shannon was all along.

She had allegedly talked to Michael Donovan at the family funeral months before and told him that she wanted to leave Craig. Reportedly, Donovan had said that she could go and stay with him, and she even had her bags packed. Karen was arrested on charges of perverting justice, and child neglect.

A neighbour told reporters that Karen had cracked after she had met with me because I was so accurate. She was frightened I could see what had really happened to her daughter.

17

As the years have gone by, I have learned to understand how my psychic guidance works when dealing with criminal cases. My guides provide me with visions of locations, glimpses of the actual crime, and surges of knowledge about the perpetrator which I now trust absolutely to be true. I know from a lifetime of psychic/medium work that the spirit world will only pass on good information, so I am confident sharing what I have learned about the Madeleine McCann case.

Madeleine McCann was allegedly snatched from a holiday-resort apartment in Portugal while her parents dined with friends 130 yards away, two days before her fourth birthday. The story made international news in May 2007. It was as if the world were holding its breath, praying for Madeleine's safe return.

I was one of those who followed the headlines, and felt anxious looking at the pictures of that little girl who smiled so sweetly. Almost as soon as the news broke, I received emails and texts from all parts of the world, asking me to find Madeleine. Many people had looked for psychics on the internet and contacted me through my website. Numerous psychics were already involved. In fact, the news media carried mentions of several of these psychics, and Gerry McCann's sister was reported to have said that psychics would have nothing to contribute. For this reason, I was at first hesitant to become involved.

Two months after Madeleine had disappeared, a businessman from Liverpool contacted me. He doesn't want me to share his identity, but I had done readings for his family members, and he believed in my psychic/medium abilities.

'Please try to find Madeleine,' he pleaded. 'Her mother Kate's family is from Liverpool.'

This man offered to fly me to Portugal and pay for my accommodation. I was to spend however much time was necessary to psychically tune into Madeleine. A neighbour of his had a contact at a British television channel, and a reporter was eager to follow me and discuss my insights on the evening news.

I was a bit wary about doing this without police or family support, but the businessman's plea touched me, and I told him I would try to draw in information. I worked out a structure for my guides in order to be able to glean the most important facts. What had happened the night Madeleine disappeared? Had she been abducted? Where was she now? I also wanted information about her abductor. Was this person from the area? Was he or she still near by?

I rested, the better to receive whatever guidance would come my way, and then settled down to psychically tune into Madeleine and her story. Almost immediately, my guides John and Alexandra showed up to assist me.

As I had learned from having worked on previous criminal cases, I sat with a pen and notepad. I projected my mind back to the night when Madeleine had gone missing and concentrated on holding on to the vision.

Almost immediately, the images started spilling in. I felt that the abductor was male and that he had got off a bus or a coach at about five o'clock on the evening of Madeleine's abduction. I saw Madeleine's father, Gerry, playing tennis that afternoon. This had been well documented in the media, and I saw it in my vision, too. I also saw the kidnapper watching Gerry from a distance.

Then I saw a woman, who looked to be in her late forties, with the abductor. I realized that she had helped with the kidnapping. She had brown hair, dark eyes and a dark complexion, and I sensed she was Portuguese-Moroccan. I was infused with the knowledge that she was one of three children and had lived with her violently abusive father for many years. On the property where she lived there was an old caravan, and the male abductor had lived in this caravan for a while. The woman had a scar on her left cheek. Her mother did not play a part in her life, but she had other family and had travelled to France to visit them.

The woman worked as a cleaner at hotels in Praia da Luz and had a strong connection with a person who lived close to the local chemist's in that city. She had also worked with children, and the priest at the church of Nossa Senhora da Luz knew her, as she had some kind of a connection with the church.

The Portuguese-Moroccan woman knew someone who worked at the resort. I saw raw meat hanging, and surmised that this employee, the one known to the woman, had somehow worked with meat at some point. He was also part of an organized paedophile network which abducts children, as were the woman and the male abductor. The resort employee noticed young Madeleine by chance and watched her for several days. He then tipped off the male abductor and the Moroccan woman that Madeleine was staying at the hotel.

Next, I was aware that these two suspects were locals in the town, and I had a strong vision that the man's details were already in the Portuguese police's database. I felt that the police knew this man, and that he had previously been arrested and incarcerated for child molestation.

The woman waited in a vehicle while the male abducted the young girl. She was supposed to transfer Madeleine to another group within the paedophile ring, but this never happened.

I knew I could draw in Madeleine's essence even if she was still alive, so I focused on doing just that. I saw an old car, maybe a Mercedes, with worn, leather seats. It seemed to date from the 1970s. I saw a flash vision of Madeleine sitting in the back seat with the woman.

The abductor drove near to the church of Nossa Senhora da Luz. Not only did the woman have a connection there but, ironically, it was also the church where the media filmed the McCanns praying for Madeleine. The male abductor was sitting four or five rows from the back of that very church while the McCanns grieved, and had visited the place more than once before.

Suddenly, I saw a clock flash in my mind with the time 10.25 on the night of the abduction. I followed the vision, which led to a small fishing boat linked to the male abductor. I also heard the word 'cockles'. The name Maria is connected either to the boat or to the area where the boat was located. Madeleine was hidden on this boat for a day and a half, and then moved elsewhere.

'Two miles inland,' I heard. It was the voice of John, my guide.

Now the car was travelling past an old school. The town had the letter 'P' in it. I saw some of Madeleine's clothing in a shallow river by a stone wall and a house.

The scene in my mind changed to that of the car rumbling down a dirt track. I saw images of clay and soil. We came to a dead end and I could see an old farmhouse made of worn, light stone with a red-tiled roof. I knew nobody lived here, but had a sense that an architect was remodelling the house. He was not connected to Madeleine's disappearance.

After that, I lost focus, and the vision. A few days later, I tried working on it again and got more visions of the house. I saw it in vivid detail, and it became etched in my memory. I felt certain that this was the house Madeleine had been taken to. It was within two miles of the resort.

The visions continued and led me to focus on the side of the house, where I saw fresh footprints and evidence of construction work. I knew that if the police found the house, I could take them to exactly where this had been done.

'Madeleine's DNA is located there,' John said. I still didn't know if Madeleine was dead or alive at that point.

DNA can be footprints, fingerprints, hair samples or even clothing.

I asked an artist friend of mine to draw the stone house. I emailed this information and the sketch of the house to the Portuguese police, but never heard back from them. I called the police in Leicester, where the McCanns live. The moment they heard the word 'psychic' they were sceptical and dismissive. Again, I emailed the information and the sketch but heard nothing in return.

In early September, Gerry and Kate McCann were named as formal suspects in their daughter's disappearance. The media exploded. This made me very emotional and frustrated. The police were allegedly claiming that samples that had been taken from the boot of the car which the McCanns had rented five weeks after Madeleine's disappearance proved that her body had been in it. I knew this was total rubbish. According to my psychic information, the McCanns had nothing to do with their daughter's disappearance. They were being falsely accused. Fortunately, these charges were later dismissed.

After a few months of silence, some images and stray thoughts started appearing to me. My guides brought up one of the McCanns' friends, Jane Tanner, who had been walking near the McCanns' apartment on the night of the abduction and had seen a man holding a child wrapped in a blanket walking away. It was reported that Tanner had essentially witnessed the abduction but had not known the child was Madeleine. She later helped police, giving them a detailed sketch of the kidnapper.

I focused on the sketch and the energy of that scene.

Instantly, I received a strong vision of Madeleine. I knew from experience that this can happen even if a person is still alive. I was tapping into Madeleine's auric field. I heard a crystal-clear voice say, 'Albanian!' and saw an image of Madeleine as she looked on the images which had been shown on television, smiling and happy. I was stunned! I was so excited to have received an identity. I had a vivid vision that her abductor was Albanian.

That opened the floodgates to a torrent of new information about the man. I zeroed in on his face and saw a slight dimple on his chin and that one of his top teeth was missing. He had large brown eyes. I visualized his unkempt hair and prolific facial hair, which has greyed significantly since the abduction. I sensed that he had had a ponytail at one time.

The information continued to flow, and I learned that the abductor had lost contact with his parents at the age of three or four. He grew up in an orphanage but has a brother and grandmother who are still alive.

I lost concentration but felt happy and content with this crucial information. My guides were quiet over the following few days. I sat down and decided to return to the sketch of the abductor, asking for more information about this person, so that the police could identify him.

The visions began immediately. I sensed that the abductor had kidnapped three children in the past. The most recent abduction before Madeleine's had been six years previously. The man had spent a total of twelve years in prison. He had served seven years on his last sentence. The man is a loner and travels with the

Portuguese-Moroccan woman in his caravan. I saw a flash of where he now lives, in the caravan, with the woman, at a caravan site. I felt he knew the area where Madeleine had been abducted. He owned four dogs, but one has since died. People in the area in which he lives call him 'the Dog Man'.

I continued to receive texts and emails begging me to find Madeleine. I carried on working on it but did not put any information out to the public.

About six months later, I psychically received new information. I learned that the Albanian was using the identity of the Portuguese-Moroccan woman's former boyfriend, and was even using his driving licence. John instructed me to zero in on the man's face, to look for identifying marks.

Suddenly, I saw a stud in the man's nostril. I felt this was highly significant, so I continued to stare at it. I also learned that the man no longer wears the stud, and the hole has healed but a scar remains. The stud was not included in Jane Tanner's eerily accurate drawing.

Next, my guides flashed me a startling vision: a penis with a slit or slice on one side. I felt it was the brand of a cult, or some kind of paedophile identity mark. I always trust the information I receive and know my guides wouldn't share anything with me that was not significant.

At the time of writing, the case of Madeleine's disappearance remains unsolved. In my opinion, the police are highly intelligent and sometimes need only the slightest bit of information to solve a case. I am neither a detective nor a scientist. I can only offer my own expertise, but I trust in it solidly enough to share it in this book.

I reveal what I have gleaned from my spirit advisors with the best intentions and only hope it can help solve the mystery of Madeleine McCann's whereabouts and offer closure to a family shattered by grief.

Epilogue

After ten years of constantly learning and testing my mediumship, I find that I continue to evolve every day. It's an ongoing process, and there is much more to explore on my path ahead.

Now I know I have a sizeable group of spirit teachers and guides who continue to help me at every stage. Everyone has a similar entourage. Some teachers pop in to help with a particular situation, then leave to assist others. Some, like Great-uncle Tom, have stayed with me for the long haul.

The stunner, Alexis, who arrived when I was first studying mediumship and gaining confidence, stayed a while and helped me with my television skills.

The priest, John, is still with me, along with the nun, Alexandra. She is kind and lovely to work with, and I consider her one of my favourite guides. John and Alexandra work together in the spirit world helping children.

Ruby is still as naughty as ever and joins me during my stage performances, feeding me advice and teasing me in his campy way. He still irritates the hell out of me, but he does make me laugh.

Giles is around me all the time and is especially helpful with private readings. He brings loved ones through. He also assists me on criminal casework.

Great-aunt Emmie shows up often, mostly to tell me off. 'You're working too hard,' she scolds. She wants me to take a break from the all-consuming life of a medium and take more time for myself. She urges me to pursue a childhood dream of acting. I thrived in secondary-school drama classes and played Robinson Crusoe in a play. I'm finally comfortable in front of a camera, so perhaps an opportunity will come my way to give me a break from mediumship.

My two children, Joseph and Maria, love and support my line of work. While Joseph is intrigued, Maria seems to have inherited my gift. She plays psychic games with her friends and can read their minds. She also has a natural awareness of people's illnesses.

My relationship with Claudine grew and flourished, and we are now engaged to be married. We are parents together to a wonderful boy, Louis. Claudine also has psychic ability, and Louis already shows great awareness and smiles at the doorway when nobody is there. Perhaps Louis will be the next generation to carry on my psychic abilities to assist mankind.

After raising ten children, my parents travel often and enjoy their lives in Standish. I am grateful to them for their role in my early gathering of knowledge.

My brother Denny visited me recently in spirit. 'Good job on the Shannon Matthews case,' he said. He was happy and relaxed with his life on the other side. He is at college there, continuing his education.

I went through a phase where people came to me for

psychic readings and wanted to know about frivolous, surface things such as money or material things or their love life.

'Will I stay with my boyfriend?' was a common question. These people wanted only good news, to keep their dramas going. I understood, because I used to be the exact same way.

'You are only seeking what you want to hear,' I told them. 'I'm picking up a male. You're in a mess and clinging to the person. You don't want to hear the truth. You want a quick fix. I could fill you with rubbish and tell you your relationship is safe but, in a few weeks, you will be in the same situation on the same merry-go-round.' I knew these people would often waste twenty years spinning in the same negative circles.

Giles, the undertaker, always stood by when I explained this to people. He began telling me how long each person had to live.

'Three years left to live,' Giles would say in the middle of a reading.

'This one has seventeen years,' he stated in another session.

This advance notice of people's death terrified me. Why was Giles giving me such frightening predictions? He did it all the time. I ignored him and did not tell anyone when to expect their death.

I thought of the old-fashioned fortune-tellers, with their crystal balls and Tarot cards. Predictions can imprint themselves on the subconscious mind and cause great damage. If people hear that they are going to die in three years' time, their own morbid thoughts can contribute towards creating that situation. Even good news can be harmful if it never comes to pass. I have come to realize that any prediction can frighten or keep people stuck in a given situation. I saw it happen to Denny after a psychic told him that he would die shortly.

Giles finally explained that, in these cases, instead of predicting what was going to happen in the future, it was better to tap into the person's aura and offer a spiritual reading instead. Giles helped me to do this by flashing me visions of the person as a child. It helped me to understand them. Maybe they had a learning disability or had grown up with an abusive parent.

'Bring this out in a constructive way,' Giles coached from the sidelines. 'Get to the root of the problem.'

Yes, that child suffered in school, struggled to read, or felt lonely and neglected by a parent. It may seem negative to focus on such things but, through reflection and learning from their experiences, the person will hopefully gain knowledge which they can, in turn, pass on to others in some way.

It was amazing to see how people responded. Instead of dwelling on a miserable past, they would recognize that they wanted to use their life experiences, however negative, to help others. In other words, this method would set them on a positive path, a way of thinking which would sustain them throughout life. This was exactly how I embarked on my own path, and began to evolve and, eventually, flourish.

The readings I was giving began to take unique twists

and turns, and I noticed people paying closer attention. I was no longer just a psychic telling someone their love life would survive or they would win the lottery and become rich and famous. I was a counsellor on earth, advancing people to a grander level in life – not through material gain, but by guiding them to their life purpose.

My life has not been easy. Mediumship, when done with honest intention, can be highly pressurized and a minefield of responsibility and expectation.

Now, my goal is to go beyond giving just messages or predictions. I want to help mend a person's spirit and set them on their own correct life path. This is the only way for humans to find true happiness.

Our light shines from within. Searching on the outside, fighting for material wealth, fame, love or happiness, has left millions of people unhappy and in deep despair.

The spark is within.

Finding that flicker of wisdom in each person will remain my life passion.

It is a gift I have been lucky enough to have been granted – and it is my gift to you.

Acknowledgements

I would like to thank my children, Joseph, Maria and my new baby son Louis, and my lovely partner Claudine for all your love and support. A special mention to Christine, Claudine's mum.

To all my family and friends, especially my Mum and Dad who have supported me over the years.

A special thank you to Jill Wellington, whose amazing talents and friendship made this book happen.

To anyone who has lost a loved one: rest assured the spirit lives on after death and the precious people you loved in life on earth are still around you.

And, finally, a special thanks to my editor, Paulette Hearn from Penguin Books for giving me this opportunity to share my story.